# Ubuntu Ethics

This book provides a philosophical exposition of Ubuntu ethics, which it does by explaining the saying 'a person is a person through other persons'. Written by one of the world's leading scholars of African philosophy, the book first argues that the focus on *umuntu* (or, a person) in Ubuntu ethics as intrinsically valuable makes ethical humanism and human dignity vitally important. The book then goes on to consider the role of virtue ethics in driving an ideal of moral perfectionism. This, in turn, provides the basis for what a good society should be: a needs-based political theory. Providing an important guide through Ubuntu ethics as a moral system constructed in terms of moral perfectionism, it will be an important read for researchers of African philosophy, and of the philosophy of virtue ethics and moral perfectionism more generally.

**Motsamai Molefe** is an Associate Professor, University of South Africa, Graduate School of Business Leadership, South Africa. He specialises in African philosophy, Ethics, and Governance. He serves as the Chair of Department: Inter-Africa Trade and Investment. He is the Editor-in-chief of the *South African Journal of Philosophy*. His recent co-authored book *African Ethics and Death: Moral Status and Human Dignity in Ubuntu Thinking* (Routledge, 2023) and co-edited book *Human Dignity in an African Context* (Palgrave, 2023).

# Routledge Studies in African Philosophy

**Feminist African Philosophy**
Women and the Politics of Difference
*Abosede Priscilla Ipadeola*

**Kimmerle's Intercultural Philosophy and Beyond**
The Ongoing Quest for Epistemic Justice
*Renate Schepen*

**African Epistemology**
Essays on Being and Knowledge
*Edited by Peter Aloysius Ikhane and Isaac E. Ukpokolo*

**African Ethics and Death**
Moral Status and Human Dignity in Ubuntu Thinking
*Motsamai Molefe and Elphus Muade*

**Intercultural Thinking in African Philosophy**
A Critical Dialogue with Kant and Foucault
*Marita Rainsborough*

**Endangered African Knowledges and the Challenge of Modernity**
An Igbo Response
*Donald Mark C. Ude*

**Ubuntu Ethics**
Human Dignity, Moral Perfectionism, and Needs
*Motsamai Molefe*

For more information about this series, please visit: https://www.routledge.com/Routledge-Studies-in-African-Philosophy/book-series/AFRPHIL

# Ubuntu Ethics
Human Dignity, Moral Perfectionism, and Needs

Motsamai Molefe

LONDON AND NEW YORK

First published 2025
by Routledge
4 Park Square, Milton Park, Abingdon, Oxon OX14 4RN

and by Routledge
605 Third Avenue, New York, NY 10158

*Routledge is an imprint of the Taylor & Francis Group, an informa business*

© 2025 Motsamai Molefe

The right of Motsamai Molefe to be identified as author of this work has been asserted in accordance with sections 77 and 78 of the Copyright, Designs and Patents Act 1988.

All rights reserved. No part of this book may be reprinted or reproduced or utilised in any form or by any electronic, mechanical, or other means, now known or hereafter invented, including photocopying and recording, or in any information storage or retrieval system, without permission in writing from the publishers.

*Trademark notice*: Product or corporate names may be trademarks or registered trademarks, and are used only for identification and explanation without intent to infringe.

*British Library Cataloguing-in-Publication Data*
A catalogue record for this book is available from the British Library

*Library of Congress Cataloging-in-Publication Data*
Names: Molefe, Motsamai, author.
Title: Ubuntu ethics : human dignity, moral perfectionism, and needs / Motsamai Molefe.
Description: Abingdon, Oxon ; New York, NY : Routledge, 2025. | Series: Routledge studies in African philosophy | Includes bibliographical references and index.
Identifiers: LCCN 2024023998 (print) | LCCN 2024023999 (ebook) | ISBN 9781032846347 (hbk) | ISBN 9781032846286 (pgk) | ISBN 9781003514213 (ebk)
Subjects: LCSH: Ubuntu (Philosophy) | Dignity. | Perfection--Moral and ethical aspects. | Ethics--Africa.
Classification: LCC B5315.U28 M67 2025 (print) | LCC B5315.U28 (ebook) | DDC 171/.2--dc23/eng/20240702
LC record available at https://lccn.loc.gov/2024023998
LC ebook record available at https://lccn.loc.gov/2024023999

ISBN: 978-1-032-84634-7 (hbk)
ISBN: 978-1-032-84628-6 (pbk)
ISBN: 978-1-003-51421-3 (ebk)

DOI: 10.4324/9781003514213

Typeset in Galliard
by KnowledgeWorks Global Ltd.

I dedicate this book to my children, Luhle, Thato, and Bohlale.

# Contents

Introduction to Ubuntu Ethics     1

1 Ubuntu Ethics, *Umuntu*, and Human Dignity     19

2 Ubuntu Ethics, *ubuntu* and Human Dignity     43

3 Ubuntu Ethics and Politics     71

*Index*     *97*

# Introduction to Ubuntu Ethics

## Introduction

The book contributes towards African moral philosophy or African ethics. To capture African ethics, it will rely on the Nguni concept of Ubuntu or, in seSotho Botho[1]. (I consider Ubuntu and Botho equivalent expressions of African ethics, but throughout the book, I will primarily use the Nguni term Ubuntu). The book will contribute towards African ethics by offering a philosophical exposition of Ubuntu as an African axiological perspective. I am mindful that there are various interpretations and approaches to Ubuntu ethics in the literature on African philosophy. Moreover, I am also aware that these interpretations differ from each other in very fundamental ways (Metz, 2007; Gade, 2011; Praeg, 2014). This book does not aim to conduct a philosophical survey, comparison, and evaluation of the plethora of Ubuntu ethics interpretations in the literature on African philosophy. The aim or task of this book is limited or moderate – it aims to offer a philosophical exposition and clarification of what it considers to be a salient interpretation of Ubuntu ethics.

The book will specifically contribute towards African ethics by proffering an exposition of Ubuntu, which the literature in African philosophy variously refers to as the *self-realisation* or *perfectionist* or *autocentric* interpretation of Ubuntu ethics (Ramose, 1999; Shutte, 2001; Metz, 2007; Van Niekerk, 2007; Molefe, 2019). Throughout the book, I will interchangeably use the terms moral perfectionism and self-realisation[2]. At the heart of the self-realisation interpretation of Ubuntu ethics is the ethical idea that each agent must develop or perfect their human nature to be characterised by a desirable character disposition (Wall, 2012). This approach to Ubuntu ethics is character-based in its orientation, where the agent's chief duty essentially involves developing a virtuous disposition (Gyekye, 2010). Moreover, I will also establish a connection between a perfectionist reading of Ubuntu ethics and the idea of human dignity. Specifically, I will account for Ubuntu ethics in terms of intrinsic and achievement dignity as its characteristic features.

DOI: 10.4324/9781003514213-1

## 2  Introduction to Ubuntu Ethics

The relevance and emergence of this book are motivated by at least two considerations. The first motivation stems from the observation that there is no book in the literature on Ubuntu ethics that is focused on systematically clarifying the nature of the perfectionist interpretation of it. Recent books on Ubuntu ethics tend to focus on different interpretations of it. For example, Leonhard Praeg's (2014) book *A Report on Ubuntu* offers what it describes as the 'critical humanism' interpretation of Ubuntu ethics. The method undergirding this book interprets philosophy as primarily a political activity. Moreover, critical humanism is an ethical and political attitude that analyses social institutions', movements', and cultures' tendency to dehumanise. In Praeg's view, ubuntu pivots on the political work it must do to undo systematic and institutional attempts to dehumanise human beings for one ideology or another[3].

Also consider Metz's (2022) book *A Relational Moral Theory: African Ethics in and Beyond the Continent*. This book proffers a relational interpretation of Ubuntu ethics, which foregrounds the relational value of friendliness, or the capacity for it, as the highest good to account for the rightness of actions[4]. On Metz's interpretation of Ubuntu ethics, the entire gamut of the enterprise of morality revolves around the value of friendliness, which Metz construes in terms of sharing a way of life and caring for others' well-being. This book differs from these in that it focuses solely on the self-realisation or perfectionist interpretation of Ubuntu ethics.

Moreover, even those books that are cognizant or even propose a self-realisation approach do not go all the way. For example, Mogobe Ramose sometimes comes across as offering a perfectionist interpretation of Ubuntu ethics. Note this comment, "... to be a human be-ing is to affirm one's humanity by recognising the humanity of others ... *One is enjoined, yes, commanded as it were, to actually become a human being*" (Ramose, 1999: 52, emphasis mine). In this reading of Ubuntu ethics, the moral agent must actually become a human being. It is not a tautology that Ramose is after by insisting that a human being that is already a human ought to actually become a human being. Rather, Ramose's reference to 'actually becoming a person' invokes the normative notion of a human being, which involves the moral agent achieving and living a true or genuine human life (Metz, 2013). The requirement to become a person suggests the agent, as a self, ought to realise his/her true moral destiny or perfect his/her human nature, which embodies a perfectionist interpretation of Ubuntu. Ramose, however, does not go on to develop a systematic elaboration of the perfectionist interpretation of Ubuntu ethics, which will clarify, amongst others, what aspect(s) of human nature is relevant for moral development and what the development of our nature would amount to and so on.

Augustine Shutte's (2001) book *Ubuntu: an Ethic for a New South Africa* is another interesting one that gestures a self-realisation or perfectionist interpretation. The major difference between this book and Shutte's book lies in several crucial philosophical points. In terms of whether Ubuntu ethics should be understood in secular or religious terms, Shutte seems to take seriously the religious interpretation of Ubuntu ethics. On my part, I propose a secular interpretation of it. I do so largely because the primary target of this book is a secular audience of philosophers and non-philosophers who might be open to learning what Ubuntu ethics might teach us about morality. A secular project is more apt for a global, democratic, and multi-cultural society. Another difference is in relation to the treatment of the concept of human dignity. In Shutte's interpretation of Ubuntu ethics, human dignity features as *seriti* (a seSotho word for dignity)[5]. He construes *seriti* as a spiritual force. Beyond the religious renderings of human dignity in the literature, the term itself of dignity is not defined, and its position in Ubuntu ethics is not systematically clarified or defended.

On my part, I will construct a philosophical picture of moral perfectionism where the concept of human dignity plays a crucial role in our aim to understand Ubuntu ethics. I will also clarify the nature of human dignity in Ubuntu ethics and its place in an African ethical system. Contrary to Shutte's treatment of human dignity, I will proffer a secular interpretation of human dignity. Shutte's book does associate Ubuntu ethics with a political system; however, it is not specific regarding the kind of political system that is most apt to capture its essence in terms of whether it is a rights-based system or invokes any other kind of fundamental value, such as utility, capabilities, needs, and so on. On my part, I will propose two related political visions revolving around the cardinal values of *human dignity* and *ubuntu*.

The second motivation for this book emerges in relation to the observation in the literature that the self-realisation interpretation is the most influential interpretation of African ethics. Surprisingly, such an influential interpretation of African ethics has not received an extensive, book-length treatment in the literature. Some may doubt that perfectionist interpretation is dominant in African ethics. Metz supports the view that the self-realisation interpretation is dominant after surveying the literature on Ubuntu ethics. He makes this remark regarding the self-realisation interpretation of Ubuntu ethics,

> This is probably *the dominant interpretation of African ethics in the literature*. Many thinkers take the maxim 'a person is a person through other persons' to be a call for an agent to develop her personhood…
>
> (Metz, 2007: 331, emphasis mine)

4  *Introduction to Ubuntu Ethics*

Metz indicates that the self-realisation interpretation of Ubuntu ethics is probably the dominant interpretation of it in the literature. There is evidence that buttresses Metz's claim that the self-realisation interpretation is dominant in the literature. The evidence for it is found in the literature on Ubuntu or the concept of personhood in African philosophy. In relation to Ubuntu, for example, Christian Gade (2012: 484) informs us that "The concept of a person is of central importance" in our quest to understand Ubuntu ethics. Moreover, an extensive body of literature interprets African ethics by focusing almost exclusively on the concept of personhood. Ifeanyi Menkiti, the famous Nigerian philosopher, was the first to offer a philosophical exposition of this concept in the literature of African philosophy (Wiredu, 2004). The idea of personhood, as used by Menkiti and all his interlocutors in the literature, tends to associate it with the self-realisation/perfectionist dimension.

For example, Menkiti (1984: 182) describes personhood as something we attain or achieve. For him, acquiring personhood involves the development of a disposition characterised by excellence. Gyekye (1992: 113) associates personhood with the "practice of virtue". Wiredu (2009: 16) understands personhood to refer "to a morally sound adult", and the designation of personhood, when used to evaluate a moral agent, is a commending term in as far as it involves the recognition and approval of the agent's conduct and deportment in relation to oneself, his/her close ties, and the community at large. Moreover, contemporary scholars of the concept of personhood, such as Metz (2013), Ikuenobe (2017), Matolino (2014), Oyowe (2018), and Molefe (2019), understand it to have this self-realisation component, where the agent is expected to acquire virtue or to lead a genuine human life. This dominant interpretation of Ubuntu ethics will be the focus of this book.

The final motivation involves who the book imagines as part of its target market. The book is written by a philosopher based in Africa. It makes sense to imagine that its primary target would be philosophers of both African and non-African descent working in philosophy in Africa or even African philosophy. The book is written with philosophers in mind who are generally interested in African ethics or philosophy in general. It aims to engage philosophers by presenting a systematic picture of Ubuntu ethics' self-realisation/perfectionist interpretation. The book is written also for philosophers unfamiliar with African philosophy or the idea of Ubuntu, but who are interested in familiarising themselves with this tradition and hopefully learning something from it and engaging it from their cultural-and-intellectual positionality. Moreover, the book hopes that it may also reach the non-philosophy audience of non-African origins or those unfamiliar with African cultures who might just be curious to understand Ubuntu ethics from the perspective of an African philosopher. I also write this book with people who want to understand the fundamentals associated with an African moral vision characteristic of African cultures below the Sahara.

In what follows, I provide the reader with an overview of the book. In the first section, I clarify the distinction between Ubuntu and *ubuntu*. The second section discusses the aim of the book. The third section focuses on methodological questions. The final section considers the structure of the book.

## Ubuntu and ubuntu

Throughout the book, I distinguish between a capitalised (Ubuntu) and a non-capitalised expression of the word (ubuntu). To differentiate between Ubuntu and ubuntu is crucial to pursue a clear and more accurate understanding of Ubuntu ethics. I am aware of two scholars who have already engaged the distinction between the capitalised and non-capitalised expression of the word Ubuntu/ubuntu, or at least it is productive to read them as making this distinction. Praeg (2014), in his book on Ubuntu, distinguishes between Ubuntu and ubuntu. According to him, if we take the differentiation concerning pre-colonial, colonial, and post-colonial epochs seriously in African thought, we can locate the capitalised Ubuntu in the pre-colonial era and the non-capitalised ubuntu in the post-colonial one. He argues that colonisation has radically severed any meaningful or successful connection or recovery of the true essence of Ubuntu as was known, experienced, and shared amongst African peoples. The violent and erasing politics of colonisation and epistemicide have destroyed any legitimate claim to Ubuntu as an axiological and cultural resource. He observes that we are only left with ubuntu. He describes ubuntu as a *glocal phenomenon*. To understand ubuntu as a glocal phenomenon involves attempting to make sense of local concepts or values by interpreting them in terms of foreign (or global) epistemic and axiological frames like Christianity, human rights, communitarianism, etc.

The idea behind Praeg's distinction between Ubuntu and ubuntu is that we will never know the true essence of Ubuntu. He further urges us to be honest concerning the political and ideological work we do when we invoke and use the concept of ubuntu in different contexts. In his view, we are using ubuntu to push our different intellectual, ideological, and political agendas by associating it with various interpretations that we prefer relative to our intellectual and political positionality. Given his positionality as a Bishop in the Christian context, Desmond Tutu associates Ubuntu with the Christian value of *agape*. In contrast, Metz, given his extensive training in the analytic tradition of philosophy, interprets it in terms of the Western *analytical techniques of philosophy*. Praeg interprets it in terms of the French philosophical school of *critical humanism*. In Praeg's view, we have no sense of Ubuntu; all we have is contesting interpretations of ubuntu, where it is a local value that is being interpreted in terms of foreign epistemic frames to give modern renditions of the value and theory of ubuntu.

I do not subscribe to Praeg's extreme scepticism concerning Ubuntu. I find the analysis of written records on Ubuntu by Christian Gade to usefully capture the distinction between Ubuntu and *ubuntu* that I deem relevant for my purposes (I italicise my use of the non-capitalised *ubuntu* to distinguish it from Praeg's use of the non-capitalised ubuntu to refer to a glocal phenomenon). Gade (2011) notes that over time, one can notice the distinction in how the term Ubuntu was used in the written records from the mid-1800s to the late 1900s. He notes that earlier, in the mid-1800s until at least around the 1970s, the term Ubuntu referred to a character trait, a virtue, or moral excellence, which was usually described in terms of humaneness. He also notes that a new tendency emerged in the 1990s, when the term was also used to refer to a worldview, cosmology, or philosophical perspective. I adopt Gade's adept observation to capture the distinction between Ubuntu and *ubuntu*[6].

The former refers to a worldview or, more accurately, an African philosophy (Ramose, 1999; Dladla, 2017). As an instance of a philosophical worldview associated with the Bantu-speaking peoples in Southern, Eastern, and Central Africa, it reflects a particular feature of their languages when they refer to a human being as *umuntu* (Nguni), *munhu* (Xitsonga), *motho* (Sotho), and so on (Eze, 2005). Ubuntu, as an African philosophical system, like any philosophical system, has its own metaphysical, epistemological, and axiological system. Its metaphysics tends to emphasise relationality as the core defining feature of reality (Magesa, 1997). Its epistemology tends to be characterised by a holistic logic. This book will focus on axiology, what I refer to as Ubuntu ethics, or simply Ubuntu.

When I use the word Ubuntu or Ubuntu ethics, I refer to a philosophical doctrine, a moral philosophy, or a moral theory. However, when I use the term *ubuntu*, I refer to the property of *umuntu* (a person). Ubuntu prescribes *ubuntu*, a Nguni term for virtue or excellence, as the chief moral goal that the moral agent ought to pursue and acquire. In this sense, *ubuntu* is something that the agent could come to obtain or have depending on the quality of her conduct, or one that he/she could fail to achieve or lose relative to defective conduct. Hence, we could talk of Ubuntu as a property of African cultures and *ubuntu* as a property of the moral agent (or a person). This analysis demonstrates that my approach is diametrically opposed to Praeg's scepticism regarding Ubuntu being altogether lost. We still have access to Ubuntu as an African ethical worldview.

One might wonder how I justify that Ubuntu has not been wholly lost to counter Praeg's argument. My argument hinges on the fact that the only condition under which Ubuntu as a philosophy could be lost entirely to African people would have been when they lost access to their African languages altogether. The argument is simple. African cultures were generally non-literate. They relied on sophisticated oral techniques to preserve knowledge. In other words, they used language itself in different ways as an archiving tool. The archiving function of language took various forms, such as songs, poetry, sayings, proverbs, and so on (Gyekye, 1995). Unsurprisingly, African philosophers of African descent, when they explain insights from their cultural contexts, would elucidate, augment, and defend their views by appealing to certain sayings and proverbs found amongst their cultures as evidence. They invoke sayings and proverbs in their exposition and argumentation because they understand these to derive value from lived-experience wisdom, philosophical insights, and important moral lessons (Dzobo, 1992). For example, Wiredu's expositions of African thought are littered with sayings and aphorisms from amongst the Akan peoples; the same goes for Gyekye, Gbadegesin, and Ramose, amongst others, as proper resources to capture African thought and provide evidence to buttress or deny certain views.

Moreover, it is also important to note that the most common and useful way to gain entrance to Ubuntu ethics is via the saying 'umuntu ngumuntu ngabantu' (Nguni languages), 'motho ke motho ka batho' (Sotho languages), or in English, 'a person is a person through other persons'. Amongst cultural insiders and those familiar with African moral cultures, the connection between the two, the concept of Ubuntu and the saying 'a person is a person through other persons', is an instinctive or intuitive one. For this reason, scholars often appeal to this saying (and others in African cultures) in their exposition of Ubuntu ethics. I will also do my philosophical exposition of the perfectionist interpretation of Ubuntu by appealing to this saying, amongst others. Hence, the persistence of African languages despite the onslaught of colonisation offers some reason to negate Praeg's claim that Ubuntu was altogether obliterated. The persisting Nguni and Sotho languages and their archiving role should bolster our belief that we still have some fragments of Ubuntu, particularly as captured via the rich linguistic 'library' of sayings and proverbs in these cultures.

Three things are worth noting about Ubuntu ethics in relation to orality. Firstly, I clarify how I understand orality in relation to African cultures and philosophy. Secondly, I clarify the connection between Ubuntu ethics and the saying 'a person is a person through other persons'. Finally, I explain my approach and understanding of the saying 'a person is a person through other persons' in terms of how I will analyse it to construct an African ethical theory.

Firstly, concerning orality, to describe Ubuntu as emerging in an oral culture that relied on oral techniques like sayings and proverbs to preserve ethical insights is a descriptive statement, which should not be wrongly interpreted to suggest that lack of writing or non-writing cultures were or are inferior to those cultures that tend to be literate. Ngugi wa Thiong'o's (2013) essay 'Tongue and Pen: a Challenge to Philosophers from Africa' makes a powerful argument regarding the relationship between a tongue and a pen. He argues that knowledge is a natural part of human functioning and culture, which he figuratively captures in terms of a *tongue*. Knowledge emerges amongst human beings, and it is not produced by pen. He further notes that the side of non-literate history is longer than that of a literate one, yet human history has never stopped because writing had not been invented as part of human culture. As much as we should value the technology of writing, we should not do so in ways that fail to properly understand it as a human aid: the pen is a human invention to preserve knowledge, it is a human being that creates or produces knowledge. Human beings, as they are, produce knowledge with or without the writing technology. Hence, Ubuntu emerged in a non-literate culture as a human activity within these cultures to make sense of the world around them in ways consistent with their cultures. It is also a welcome addition to discourses on Ubuntu that it now has an extensive and rich written archive.

Secondly, Gade, in his historical analysis of the concept of Ubuntu, makes a fascinating discovery regarding the relation between Ubuntu and the saying 'a person is a person through other persons'. Gade (2011: 302) notes,

> Furthermore, my findings indicate that it was during the period from 1993 to 1995 that the Nguni proverb' *umuntu ngumuntu ngabantu*' (often translated as 'a person is a person through other persons') was used for the first time to describe what *ubuntu* is.

It is important to clarify that this conclusion should be appreciated in the context of the historical analysis of written texts on Ubuntu in English. Regarding the historical analysis of written texts, it might well be true that the connection only emerges in the written archive between 1993 and 1995. The fact of the matter is that the written archive was very late to arrive at such a basic and intuitive connection amongst cultural insiders below the Sahara concerning Ubuntu and the saying 'a person is a person through other persons'. From the youngest person to the oldest amongst African communities, the connection between Ubuntu and the saying *'umuntu ngumuntu ngabantu'* is overt and obvious even if the individuals may not have pondered the meaning of the connection between the word Ubuntu and the saying, or even of the deep meaning of the saying itself. As a cultural insider, when I first encountered Ubuntu in the written discourses around 2007 at the University of the Witwatersrand, I was already aware of the connection between Ubuntu and the saying 'a person is a person through other person', and my mother who had taught me this saying, who was non-literate, was aware of this connection. The book relies on this connection between Ubuntu ethics and the saying 'umuntu ngumuntu ngabantu' to explain it, and it will construe it on a perfectionist frame.

Finally, my exposition of Ubuntu ethics relies on the saying 'a person is a person through other persons'. In my approach, I divide the phrase into three components that revolve around the concept of a *person*: (a) a person, (b) is a person, (c) through other persons. I believe that correctly interpreting these three constitutive components of the saying would give us a correct understanding of Ubuntu ethics. For starters, it is worth noting that the concept of *umuntu* or a person is central in Ubuntu ethics, which suggests that to grasp Ubuntu ethics, we should pay special attention to it as it appears in the saying (Gade, 2011). As the reader will note in the coming chapters, the values central in Ubuntu ethics are based and derived from the concepts of personhood as expressed in the saying.

Next, I turn to the aim of the book.

## The Aim of the Book

The book aims to offer a philosophical explication of Ubuntu ethics. It mainly aims to limit its focus on Ubuntu ethics when construed as a self-realisation/perfectionist theory of value. It is not an exaggeration to suggest that Ubuntu can be understood as an essentially contested notion – there are as many interpretations of it as there are theoreticians of it (see Molefe, 2019). For example, Metz (2007), in his essay 'Towards an African Moral Theory', identifies at least six differing and competing interpretations of Ubuntu ethics as a theory of right action. These theories differ fundamentally in terms of the value(s) they prescribe as fundamental to capture Ubuntu ethics – life, dignity, well-being, rights, self-realisation, survival, and community. Other scholars associate Ubuntu with *seriti* (Shutte, 1993), harmony (Tutu, 1999), critical humanism (Praeg, 2014), love (Tshivhase, 2018), and so on. The aim of the book is not to explore this large swathe of literature on Ubuntu ethics. Instead, the exposition anticipated here aims to make three significant theoretical clarifications and contributions to the perfectionist interpretations of Ubuntu ethics.

The exposition aims (a) to place significance on *umuntu* or a person as the primary or foundational moral consideration in Ubuntu ethics. The exposition (b) seeks to reveal the self-and-other regarding aspects of *ubuntu* as a virtue, where the agent's duty to perfect herself is understood as enmeshed with/in (the) community or its good. Finally, the exposition will intervene (c) by associating Ubuntu ethics with a political approach that prizes non-humiliation, on the one hand, and the common good (basic needs), on the other hand, as the basis for a decent or good society.

In relation to (a), the literature has tended to focus on *umuntu*, or a person, as the agent that has a duty to perfect herself as the primary moral consideration (Menkiti, 1984; Tutu, 1999; Mokgoro, 1999). The tendency in the literature is to believe that the agent's goal to become a person or to have a *ubuntu* exhausts Ubuntu ethics. The intervention related to (a) proposes that it is the agent, as *umuntu*, a human being, as he/she is, without doing anything in the world, that is the primary holder or possessor of value that a correct interpretation of Ubuntu ethics must reckon with. The call by (a) is that we must recognise *umuntu* (or, a person) as a bearer of intrinsic value. The intervention associated with (a) proposes that dignity is the primary and central value in Ubuntu ethics – *umuntu* is a bearer of dignity.

In relation to (b), the literature has tended to think of *ubuntu* in terms of over-emphasising the community and communal values to the extent of almost overlooking the individual and individual values. It is common in African philosophy to come across the idea that the community takes priority over the individual (Menkiti, 1984; Nkondo, 2007). To counteract this tendency, (b) proposes an interpretation of the self-realisation account of Ubuntu ethics that recognises both the self-regarding and other-regarding aspects of value. The intervention associated with (b) points to the fact that there are some aspects of the individual, her/his human nature, that the agent must cultivate in order to acquire *ubuntu* or virtue, which is an individualistic consideration. However, the agent can only cultivate or acquire virtue in robust interpersonal relationships – the self-regarding duty of personal perfection is intrinsically married to the communitarian orientation to place emphasis on relationships, social values, and the common good.

In relation to (c), the literature has tended to associate Ubuntu ethics with human rights (Wiredu, 1996; Gyekye, 1997; Metz, 2012; Matolino, 2014; Oyowe, 2014). The intervention by (c) indicates that needs, construed in terms of the common good or the human minimum, are much more at home in Ubuntu ethics than considerations associated with human rights. A good society recognises human dignity by removing conditions that humiliate citizens and one that provides basic needs that are required for human agents to flourish. I believe that these three interventions in the literature on Ubuntu interpreted as a perfectionist/self-realisation theory of value promises to offer a clearer picture of it. This systematic exposition of the perfectionist interpretation will be useful to distinguish it from other interpretations of Ubuntu ethics and it can also serve as the basis to compare it against other self-realising (or perfectionist) value theories from other traditions of philosophy like some interpretations of Confucianism or virtue ethics in the west.

## Questions of Method

Concerning methodology, I consider two crucial issues: the use of the moniker 'African' and the philosophical method I will use to facilitate an exposition of Ubuntu ethics.

### *The Term Africa*

I begin with the use of the term Africa. The term Africa can sometimes cause confusion when its use is not carefully clarified, contextualised, and justified. Mogobe Ramose's philosophical reflection on the term Africa will be helpful as a guide to how I use it in the book. In the essay titled 'I Doubt, Therefore African Philosophy Exists', Ramose (2003) offers the history of the origins of the term Africa, its meaning in the context of clarifying the nature of African philosophy, and justifies why we should continue to use it. Ramose remarks as follows regarding (2003: 118) the origins of the term Africa,

> It has emerged in the course of our considerations above that the term 'African' is of Greek and Roman origin. It does not arise from the indigenous conquered inhabitants of the continent.
> 
> (Africa)

The name Africa was coined and used to refer to this place by Westerners, and its primary reference or meaning focused on the weather conditions. Ramose's concern regarding the use and meaning of the term is that it does not take cognisance of the people and their cultures; rather, it overlooks them to focus on the weather conditions, which use of the term slights the dignity of the people of this place. Moreover, Ramose notes that the name of the place Africa was not coined by Africans, and its use and meaning tend to exclude them since its focus is on the weather conditions. He goes on to argue that these considerations are not sufficient to secure the claim that we should repudiate the name.

Ramose proposes that we should espouse the name and use it to identify ourselves as people of the continent. When we do so, however, we should take it upon ourselves to define it or to give content to it. The project of retaining and providing content to the name Africa is a crucial, ethical, and political one that requires urgent attention. The project of keeping the name and giving new content has both negative and positive components. The negative project involves rejecting all arbitrary and external impositions that aim to degrade our humanity, our cultures, and our home Africa. The project is not one of rejecting even positive contributions from other cultures and peoples. In fact, positive contributions and borrowings characterised by dialogue and mutual exchanges amongst cultures are welcome and necessary for human development. The positive part of the project pivots on the important value and ideology of self-determination, where African peoples become the captain of their identity, mission, and destiny as they navigate their place in the world.

Caution is necessary, however, when we retain the term Africa. We must shun all the forms romanticising and essentialising it when we choose to take the term seriously. We will not operate with the romantic picture that everything labelled African is perfect and excellent. We should be cautious of tendencies to misrepresent the place Africa, its peoples and its cultures. This tendency often takes the form of portraying Africa as homogenous, which approach obscures the diversity, dynamicity and complexity of this place, its peoples and cultures. This simplistic approach often has dehumanising and degrading consequences for the dignity of the people and their cultures. Africans must be regarded as human, and they do all that any human being from any community can do – you will find saints, soldiers, politicians, criminals, heroes, kings and so on. Moreover, I reasonably use the term Africa to negotiate the intersection of thought and place, which I understand to represent the moment for creativity in the demanding journey to self-define-and-determine. If plurality, complexity, and dynamicity, amongst others, become our point of departure in the provision of content for the term Africa, it should be expected that the term Africa will always have contested dimensions, as we debate it from our different vantage points in relation to the meanings we can associate with it. What Ramose describes as 'a *struggle* for reason', which involves the task to self-define-and-determine should be understood as a struggle precisely because it (the term Africa) perennially has the contested element as an essential part of it.

With this sketch concerning the term Africa, we can consider two common and plausible uses of the term Africa in African philosophy (Oyowe, 2014; Ikuenobe, 2016). Oritsegbubemi Oyowe (2014: 333) explains the two meanings of the term Africa as follows: "One picks out a geographical category merely while the other refers to a family of ideas distinctive of cultures in the geographical area denoted as Africa". The term Africa refers to a place occupied by a people with its own experiences, histories, and cultures. A place can be located on the map. The second meaning of the term African identifies 'a family of ideas distinctive of cultures' in a place. The second meaning suggests that places have both elements of diversity within them and those of commonalities, and Oyowe refers to the commonalities as a 'family of ideas distinctive' to Africa.

Metz (2010: 52) identifies the following as an example of the basket of ideas distinctive to Africa –

> indigenous sub-Saharans often think that society should be akin to family; they typically refer to people outside the nuclear family with titles such as 'sisi' and 'mama'; they tend to believe in the moral

importance of greetings, even to strangers; they usually think that there is some obligation to wed and procreate; they generally say that 'charity begins at home' or that 'family comes first'; they frequently believe that ritual and tradition have a certain degree of moral significance; they usually do not believe that retribution is a proper aim of criminal justice, inclining toward reconciliation; they commonly think that there is a strong duty for the rich to aid the poor; and they often value consensus in decision-making, seeking unanimous agreement and not resting content with majority rule. I have the space merely to suggest that these recurrent values are plausibly entailed and well explained by the prescription to respect relationships in which people both share a way of life and care for one another's quality of life.

To claim that some idea(s) is 'distinctive' in Africa is not the same as to claim that it occurs everywhere and solely in it. Instead, it denotes their prominence in Africa, as compared to other places (Metz, 2007). I will be using the idea of Africa to refer to both a place on a map and the family of ideas salient in it guided by the literature and my experience in the place Africa (Oyowe, 2014). Ubuntu is one such salient moral category that captures moral and ethical perspectives amongst African peoples and cultures, which is the focus of this book (Eze, 2005; LenkaBula, 2009).

*African Analytical Philosophy*

I now proceed to describe the method I will use to carry out the philosophical exposition of Ubuntu ethics. I locate this book in the body of work that contributes to what I describe as African analytical philosophy. I employ the phrase 'African analytical philosophy' to refer to scholars who use the analytic method of doing philosophy in the context of African philosophy. There is a growing body of work that tends to use the techniques of analytic philosophy in the context of African philosophy (Wiredu, 1980, 1996; Gyekye, 1995, 1997; Matolino, 2014, 2019; Molefe, 2019, 2021; Oyowe, 2021; Metz, 2022; Aribiah, 2022). The techniques of analytical philosophy are typically characterised by two features: linguistic or conceptual analysis and argumentation (Molefe, 2015). Language, specifically concepts, serves as a tool through which we make sense of the world. Concepts allow us to search and construct meaning and truth. Concepts afford us an opportunity to describe and attach values to things in the world. Linguistic or conceptual analysis involves breaking down concepts into their elements in order to understand, define, and use them correctly in the quest for clarity in meaning and to approximate the truth (Swift, 2009).

If we do not use language correctly, we may never be able to properly grasp the world's issues, problems, and puzzles, which may serve as an obstacle to our quest for the truth. The assertion by Gyekye (1992: 242–243) is illuminating concerning what conceptual analysis involves –

> For philosophy is a conceptual response to the problems posed in any given epoch for a given society. It is therefore appropriate, even imperative, for contemporary African philosophers to grapple at the conceptual level with the problems and issues of their times, not least of which are the problems of government and political stability.

Gyekye construes philosophy as a conceptual response whose primary service involves dispelling confusions and unclarities in relation to issues occasioned by human experiences. If the concept of Ubuntu is central in our search for the values and goals it espouses for a decent society then philosophy as a conceptual response would involve breaking this concept into constituent elements to understand it correctly and clearly define it, and to deploy it further to make sense of the moral world.

Often, doing philosophy involves more than just the clarity of ideas and issues; it also consists of providing reasons or evidence to support or justify one's claims/views – this refers to the aspect of argumentation. An argument essentially involves justifying one's claims or providing reasons for why we should take a particular view seriously. A view, claim, or theory is plausible to the extent that it has rational credibility, i.e., sufficient reasons support it. The stronger the reasons in favour of a claim, the more we have a basis to accept it as plausible. However, if the reasons justifying a particular claim are less than sufficient, we have a solid basis to reject it. Reasons are the currency that philosophers accept as the standard of acceptability or plausibility of claims. Metz (2007: 378) exemplifies how plausibility (via a quality of reason) works in the analytic tradition:

> ... the method of positing of a general principle, posing a particular counterexample, reformulating the general principle to avoid the counterexample, posing a new counterexample to the reformulated principle, revising the principle yet again, and so on. That is the kind of methodology I have in mind when I speak of seeking to achieve my aim in a 'systematic, analytic way'...

The aim of the argumentative aspect involves testing a claim against counterclaims. The more a claim can address the concerns of the counterclaim, the more plausible we may consider it to be, and the opposite is also true.

Now that we have noted that the techniques of analytic philosophy are characterised by conceptual analysis and argumentation, I wish to make one final submission concerning this book. The book leans more on the side of conceptual analysis than on the side of argumentation.

Remember, the aim of the book essentially consists of a philosophical exposition of Ubuntu ethics, which will involve systematically clarifying the nature of Ubuntu ethics as a self-realisation or perfectionist interpretation of value. Though the goal is not argumentative, I will attempt to provide as plausible an account of Ubuntu ethics as is possible. Though the burden of this book is not so much to defend a plausible interpretation of Ubuntu ethics, it does not follow that it will not attempt to offer as reasonable, if not a plausible, account of the perfectionist interpretation of Ubuntu ethics as is possible[7].

Below, I consider the structure of the book.

## The Structure of the Book

The structure of the book mirrors the stated aims of the book, which involve three interventions in relation to the exposition of Ubuntu ethics. Remember, the first intervention involves recognising the primacy of *umuntu* (or a person) in Ubuntu ethics. The first chapter will present Ubuntu ethics as an ethics of dignity, where the primary moral value revolves around the human being as a moral patient. Human dignity implies a human being, as he/she is in the world before becoming or doing anything, she possesses inalienable and superlative value. The chapter deals with intrinsic value. Remember, the second intervention involves the concept of *ubuntu*, which refers to virtue or excellence. The second chapter will give an account of Ubuntu as an instance of moral perfectionism/self-realisation theory in African thought. Amongst others, the chapter will unfold the self-and-other-regarding facets of virtue associated with *ubuntu* as the final good. The second chapter focuses on the final good. The third and final intervention focuses on political theory. It asks which approach to politics is most apt and compatible with Ubuntu ethics. The chapter aims to answer this question by proposing a dual political model tethered to the twin values of human dignity and *ubuntu*, where the former demands overall conditions of existence that are not humiliating, and the latter requires pre-conditions in the form of basic needs, which are necessary for the emergence of a robust agent that can pursue *ubuntu*. The final chapter appeals to the values of humiliation and needs to construct an African political theory.

## Notes

1 There are other important concepts to explore and elucidate African ethics in the literature in African philosophy. Concepts like *ukama*, *isithunzi*, and *ezumezu*, amongst others. In my estimation, they are not as influential as Ubuntu in the literature. These concepts will not feature in this book because it is solely approaching African ethics through the lenses of Ubuntu as a moral perspective.

2  In Chapter 2, I will clarify the difference between the two uses, though both moral terms imagine a moral view that requires personal development as the core defining feature of ethics. The difference lies in that the latter presupposes moral egoism as a feature of the kind of moral perfectionism associated with Ubuntu ethics.
3  The non-capitalised ubuntu in this instance is distinct from the one that is the focus of my own interpretation of Ubuntu ethics, which I will italicise. I will distinguish my own use of *ubuntu* by italicising.
4  Initially, Metz's interpretation of Ubuntu ethics considered harmonious or friendly relations to be intrinsically valuable. In his latest work, however, he interprets Ubuntu ethics to posit the capacity for harmonious relationships or friendliness to be intrinsically valuable (Metz, 2007, 2017, 2022).
5  *Seriti* is an African word/concept for dignity. The word denotes a shadow or gravitas. Metz (2012) and Molefe (2022) offer a powerful philosophical exposition of this religious interpretation of human dignity.
6  To distinguish my lower-case use of the word ubuntu from Praeg's one that refers to a global phenomenon, I will italicise mine. Whereas his refers to a particular approach and view of Ubuntu ethics, mine refers to a virtue or excellence associated with the moral agent.
7  I do anticipate the objector correctly noting that the analytic technique of philosophy has a Western origin, and if I classify this project as a contribution to African thought then I should altogether abandon the analytic technique of philosophy. Two reasons justify why I personally insist on the analytic techniques of philosophising. The first reason points the objector to the plethora of work under this rubric, done by African scholars that Are committed to both Africa and to thought as a mode of doing philosophy. I am the first to admit that this is not the only method to do African philosophy, but I choose to add my voice in the literature amongst those who prefer this technique which is a big community that one cannot easily wish away. The second reason recognises the intuitive appeal inherent in the techniques of analytic philosophy. The idea of properly using language and concepts to represent and understand issues is common amongst all cultures. If we do not do linguistic or conceptual analysis, how shall we be clear and precise on matters or questions before us? Moreover, the requirement to provide reasons or justify our claims or positions is universal to all cultures. Surely, if ours is a struggle for reason, as Ramose describes it, it does imply that we are committed to reason as a standard of validity or truth. Hence, the proper use of language and argument as a criterion of engagement is ultimately a human activity of pursuing and defending the validity of claims. It is a contingent feature of the technique of analytic philosophy that it emerged in a particular form in the Western tradition, or so we believe.

## References

Aribiah, D. (2022). *Groundwork for a New Kind of African Metaphysics*. New York, NY: Palgrave Macmillan.

Dladla, N. (2017). Towards an African Critical Philosophy of Race: Ubuntu as a Philo-Praxis of Liberation. *Filosofia Theoretica* 6: 117–225.

Dzobo, N. (1992). Values in a Changing Society: Man, Ancestors, and God. In K. Wiredu and K. Gyekye (Eds.), *Person and Community: Ghanaian Philosophical Studies*, vol. I. Washington, DC: Council for Research in Values and Philosophy, 223–400.

Eze, O. (2005). *Ubuntu: A Communitarian Response to Liberal Individualism.* Pretoria: University of Pretoria.

Gade, C. (2011). The Historical Development of the Written Discourses on Ubuntu. *South African Journal of Philosophy* 30: 303–329.

Gade, C. (2012). What is Ubuntu: Different Interpretations Among South Africans of African Descent. *South African Journal of Philosophy* 31: 484–503.

Gyekye, K. (1992). Person and Community: Ghanaian Philosophical Studies, 1. Washington, DC: Council for Research in Values and Philosophy.

Gyekye, K. (1995). *An Essay on African Philosophical Thought: The Akan Conceptual Scheme.* Philadelphia, PA: Temple University Press.

Gyekye, K. (1997). *Tradition and Modernity: Philosophical Reflections on the African Experience.* New York, NY: Oxford University Press.

Gyekye, K. (2010). African Ethics. In E. N. Zalta (Ed.). *The Stanford Encyclopedia of Philosophy.* Accessed 16 January 2013. http://plato.stanford.edu/archives/fall2011/entries/african-ethics.

Ikuenobe, P. (2016). Good and Beautiful: A Moral-Aesthetic View of Personhood in African Communal Traditions. *Essays in Philosophy* 17: 124–163.

Ikuenobe, P. (2017). The Communal Basis for Moral Dignity: An African Perspective. *Philosophical Papers* 45: 437–469.

LenkaBula, P. (2009). Beyond Anthropocentricity-Botho/Ubuntu and the Quest for Economic and Ecological Justice. *Religion and Theology* 15: 375–394.

Magesa, L. (1997). *African Religion: The Moral Traditions of Abundant Life.* New York, NY: Orbis Books.

Matolino, B. (2014). *Personhood in African Philosophy.* Pietermaritzburg: Cluster Publications.

Matolino, B. (2019). Consensus as Democracy. Grahamstown. NISC (Pty)LTD.

Menkiti, I. (1984). Person and Community in African Traditional Thought. In R. A. Wright (Ed.), *African Philosophy: An Introduction.* Lanham. Lanham: University Press of America, 171–181.

Metz, T. (2007). Toward an African Moral Theory. *The Journal of Political Philosophy* 15: 321–341.

Metz, T. (2010). Human Dignity, Capital Punishment and an African Moral Theory: Toward a New Philosophy of Human Rights. *Journal of Human Rights* 9: 81–99.

Metz, T. (2012). An African Theory of Moral Status: A Relational Alternative to Individualism and Holism. *Ethical Theory and Moral Practice: An International Forum* 14: 387–402.

Metz, T. (2013). Two Conceptions of African Ethics in the Work of D. A. Masolo. *Quest* 25: 7–15.

Metz, T. (2016). An Ubuntu-based Evaluation of the South African State's Responses to Marikana: Where's the Reconciliation? *Politikon,* 44(2): 287–303.

Metz, T. (2022). *A Relational Moral Theory: African Ethics in and Beyond the Continent.* Oxford: Oxford University Press.

Mokgoro, Y. (1999). Ubuntu and the Law in South Africa. *Potchefstroom Electronic Law Journal* 1: 1–11.

Molefe, M. (2015). A Rejection of Humanism in African Moral Tradition. *Theoria* 62: 59–77.

Molefe, M. (2019). *An African Philosophy of Personhood, Morality and Politics.* New York, NY: Palgrave Macmillan.

Molefe, M. (2021). *Partiality and Impartiality in African Philosophy*. New York, NY: Lexington Books.
Molefe, M. (2022). *Human Dignity in African Philosophy: A Very Short Introduction*. New York, NY: Springer.
Nkondo, G. (2007). Ubuntu as a Public Policy in South Africa: A Conceptual Framework. *International Journal of African Renaissance Studies* 2: 88–100.
Oyowe, A. (2014). Fiction, Culture and the Concept of a Person. *Research in African Literatures* 45: 46–62.
Oyowe, A. (2018). Personhood and Strong Normative Constraints. *Philosophy East & West* 68: 783–801.
Oyowe, A. (2021). *Menkiti's Moral Man*. Lanham, MD: Lexington Books.
Praeg, L. (2014). *A Report on Ubuntu*. Pietermaritzburg: University of KwaZulu of Press.
Ramose, M. (1999). *African Philosophy Through Ubuntu*. Harare: Mond Books.
Ramose, M. (2003). I Doubt, Therefore African Philosophy Exists. *South African Journal of Philosophy* 22: 113–127.
Shutte, A. (1993). *Philosophy for Africa*. Rondebosch: University of Cape Town Press.
Shutte, A. (2001). *Ubuntu: An Ethic for a New South Africa*. Pietermaritzburg: Cluster Publications.
Swift, A. (2009). *Political Philosophy: A Beginners' Guide for Students and Politicians*. Cambridge: Polity Press.
Thiong'o, N. (2013). Tongue and Pen: A Challenge to Philosophers from Africa a Translation of 'Rūrīmī na karamu: ithoga harĩ athamaki a Abirika'. *Journal of African Cultural Studies* 25: 158–163.
Tshivhase, M. (2018). Love as the Foundation of Ubuntu. *Synthesis Philosophica* 65: 197–208.
Tutu, D. (1999). *No Future Without Forgiveness*. New York, NY: Random House.
Van Niekerk, J. (2007). In Defence of an Autocentric Account of Ubuntu. *South African Journal of Philosophy* 26: 364–368.
Wall, S. (2012). Perfectionism in Moral and Political Philosophy. Stanford Encyclopaedia of Philosophy. http://plato.stanford.edu/archives/win2012/entries/perfectionism-moral.
Wiredu, K. (1980). *Philosophy and an African Culture*. Cambridge: Cambridge University Press.
Wiredu, K. (1996). *Cultural Universals and Particulars: An African Perspective*. Indianapolis, IN: Indiana University Press.
Wiredu, K. (2004). Introduction: African Philosophy in Our Time. In K. Wiredu (Ed.), *Companion to African Philosophy*. Oxford: Blackwell Publishing, 1–27.
Wiredu, K. (2009). An Oral Philosophy of Personhood: Comments on Philosophy and Orality. *Research in African Literatures* 40: 8–18.

# 1 Ubuntu Ethics, *Umuntu*, and Human Dignity

## Introduction

What is the foundational or building block of Ubuntu ethics? Another way to think about this question is in terms of drawing a distinction between what I describe as *primary* and *secondary* values. A 'primary value' refers to what philosophers usually describe as the 'ultimate value', which, when conceived in terms of the analogy of a building, we can think of as the foundation of a building or a house (Kymlicka, 1990; Goulet, [1996] 1997). A value is primary or ultimate as far as all other values can be reduced to it, or all other values depend on it and/or are instrumentally supportive of it. For example, hedonistic utilitarianism posits pleasure as the ultimate good, and all other values, whether well-being or freedom, depend on and support it. In other words, well-being in and of itself has no value unless it is connected somehow with pleasure. 'Secondary values', on the other hand, support the ultimate or primary value like knowledge. In line with the analogy of a building, we can think of the secondary value as a superstructure that depends on the foundation.

The chapter aims to philosophically unfold the primary or foundational value characteristic of Ubuntu as a moral perspective. In more precise terms, the aim involves systematically specifying and elaborating the ultimate value grounding an African axiological system characteristic of Ubuntu ethics. Ultimately, this chapter will associate the primary or ultimate value with *umuntu* (a person). The understanding that will emerge will construe *umuntu*, a person, or a human being, as the bearer of intrinsic value[1]. *Umuntu*, a human being, a specific ontological kind, *homo sapiens*, are bearers of intrinsic value, which denotes that they are beings of dignity. The primary value definitive of Ubuntu ethics is that of human dignity, where I construe *umuntu* as a bearer of this value.

To approach the subject of the ultimate value in the exposition of Ubuntu ethics, I remind the reader that our analysis draws from the saying *umuntu ngumuntu ngabantu* (Nguni languages), *motho ke motho ka botho* (seSotho languages), or in English, 'a person is a person through other persons'. The word *umuntu, motho*, or a person occurs three times in the saying. I propose that to make headway in fulfilling the task of unfolding the ultimate value characteristic of Ubuntu ethics, it is crucial that we understand the concept(s) of a person (or, *umuntu*) and their significance in African thought. My analysis of the saying constitutive of Ubuntu ethics involves breaking it into three distinct components, namely, (a) a person, (b) is a person, and (c) through other persons. These three components constitute the moral vision and wisdom of Ubuntu ethics. Each of these components contains the word person, wherein each use of the word person carries with it a different concept of it – I will come back to this point below. I emphasise, however, the crucial place and meaning associated with the concepts of *umuntu*, or a person, in Ubuntu ethics. It is these different concepts of a person, as expressed in the components (a), (b), and (c), that will help us to identify and understand the values, the primary and secondary, of Ubuntu ethics.

This chapter will focus on the primary value definitive of Ubuntu ethics, which is associated with the first component of the saying '*a person* is a person through other persons'. The next chapter will focus on the second component, 'a person *is a person* through other persons', which captures the value of *ubuntu* that I consider the secondary value. The focus on *umuntu*, or a person, as captured in the first component, is crucial for two significant reasons. Firstly, it will help us, as indicated above, to identify, distinguish, and explain the different concepts of a person in African philosophy. When we are armed with clarity regarding the concepts of a person in African thought, we can intervene decisively in our attempts to properly understand Ubuntu ethics, mainly if our aim involves clarifying the ultimate value that lies at its core.

Secondly, one of the crucial philosophical interventions in the literature on Ubuntu ethics will involve rethinking and possibly clarifying the relationship between *umuntu* and *ubuntu*. To clarify the relationship between *umuntu* and *ubuntu*, I will rely on the analysis of the saying 'umuntu ngumuntu ngabantu' or 'a person is a person through other persons', particularly focusing on its components that a demarcated by the word/concept person. The first instance of the word *umuntu*/person in the opening phrase 'a person', or *umuntu* in the Nguni rendition, captures the primary value of Ubuntu ethics. The second instance of the word *umuntu*/person in the phrase 'is a person', or *ngumuntu* in the Nguni rendition, refers to *ubuntu*, a moral disposition characterised by virtue/excellence, which I will construe as a secondary value. I propose that we consider the two, *umuntu* and *ubuntu*, as interdependent values of a single moral vision. However, in this chapter, I will indicate and argue that *umuntu* is prior and primary in an African ethical vision as the foundation and *ubuntu* is a superstructure that depends on the former[2].

This chapter is important in that it corrects the tendency in the interpretation of Ubuntu ethics to emphasise *ubuntu* at the expense of potentially neglecting the importance of *umuntu* in value theory in African thought. If it is true that *umuntu* embodies a particular value and *ubuntu* also embodies a value, it then becomes philosophically urgent that we clarify where we ought to locate the ultimate value. I will argue that we associate the primary value on the concept of *umuntu*. Moreover, as part of correcting the excesses associated with the tendency to focus on *ubuntu* in the literature (which involves the moral agent acquiring virtue), this chapter will intervene by associating *umuntu* with the value of human dignity. The move to associate *umuntu* with human dignity will be crucial in the literature on Ubuntu ethics. A vast body of literature on Ubuntu ethics does not directly connect *umuntu* and human dignity (Bujo, 2001; Murove, 2007; Nkondo, 2007; Lutz, 2009). There is, however, literature that anticipates the relationship between *umuntu* and human dignity (Wiredu, 1996; Gyekye, 1997; Ilesanmi, 2001). However, this literature is unclear regarding the meaning, place, and role of human dignity in African ethics. This chapter aims to shed light on the relationship between *umuntu* and human dignity, and it will further clarify the nature and place of human dignity in Ubuntu ethics. Clarifying the relationship between *umuntu* and human dignity is crucial as it will explain how *umuntu* captures the ultimate or foundational value in Ubuntu ethics.

The aim of this chapter involves explicating the primary value characteristic of Ubuntu ethics. The chapter is interpretive and expository in its orientation. This chapter does not aim to argue that the picture of Ubuntu ethics that it will provide is the most plausible conception of it in the literature. Rather, this chapter's aim is limited, which involves explaining Ubuntu ethics as embodying a perfectionist vision of morality. As much as the aim, the chapter is not an argumentative one (i.e., I do not aim to defend the perfectionist view as the most plausible interpretation of Ubuntu ethics). I will, however, attempt to offer as compelling an account of Ubuntu ethics as possible given the aims and limitations of the book.

I structure the chapter as follows. The first section will distinguish the various concepts of personhood and meanings associated with them in African philosophy. The aim of the analysis of the various concepts of personhood involves explaining the saying, 'a *person* is a *person* through other *persons*', in relation to the concepts of personhood characteristic of it. This section will associate the phrase 'a person' with both the ontological notion of a person and the patient-centred normative notion of a person. It will associate the phrase 'is a person' with the agent-centred normative concept of a person[3]. The second section distinguishes between the intrinsic and final good. It will associate the concept of *umuntu*, as found in the first phrase, 'a person', with intrinsic value, and it will proceed to account for *umuntu* (a person) captured in terms of intrinsic value, in terms of human dignity. In relation to human dignity, I will (a) define the concept of human dignity, (b) explain its centrality in African thought, and (c) propose an account of human dignity that can be associated with Ubuntu ethics.

## Ubuntu Ethics and the Concepts of Personhood

The saying constitutive of the moral wisdom associated with Ubuntu ethics echoes the importance of *umuntu* or a person in African thought. The saying comprises three instances of the word person: (a) a person, (b) is a person, and (c) through other persons. To understand the saying, it is important to clarify the various senses of the word person in African thought. I identify at least four distinct concepts of a person in African thought, two of them ontological and another two normative, namely, personhood as (a) the ontological fact of being human and (b) the ontological concept of personal identity, and (c) the idea of moral status and/or (human) dignity and (d) the idea of virtue or excellence (see Molefe, 2018, 2019, 2021)[4]. The most common distinction in African philosophy often points to the difference between the ontological and normative concepts of a person. For example, Kwasi Wiredu (1996: 159) captures this distinction in this fashion:

> In one sense the Akan word *onipa* translates into the English word *person* in the sense of human being, the possessor of *okra*, *mogya*, and *sunsum*. In this sense everyone is born a person, an onipa. This is the descriptive sense of the word. But there is a further sense of the word *onipa* in which to call an individual a person is to commend him; it implies a recognition that s/he has attained a certain status in the community.

The ontological concept refers to being human, a class of ontological beings characterised by certain descriptive features like the body and/or soul (Ikuenobe, 2016). To be a person in the ontological sense, it is sufficient that one is born of human parentage. On the other hand, the normative notion refers to an agent that has lived up to a certain standard of excellence. To be called a person in this sense essentially involves being approved and praised for having led a choice-worthy or excellent life. In simple terms, when used normatively, the designation of a person denotes virtue, where the agent under consideration has been able to develop a virtuous disposition and deportment. Note that the ontological notion of a person merely refers to the status of being human, which we have by simply being the kind of a thing we are. We do not earn or acquire this status; it is a biological given because we are born into a human family.

At the same time, the normative notion imagines a moral agent that must pursue and acquire virtue. One cannot fail at being a person in the ontological sense, but one can fail to be a person in the normative sense.

To leave matters at the level of distinguishing the ontological from the normative notion of a person is a good starting point. Still, it does not provide us with a more precise and fuller picture of the issues in relation to the concept of personhood and/or African ethics. To give a clearer understanding of the concepts of personhood, we should further identify another ontological and normative notions of a person. We have noted the ontological notion that refers to the fact of being human. There is another ontological notion of personhood, which captures the concept of *personal identity*. The idea of personal identity involves, amongst others, reflecting on questions such as "… at what point in our development from a fertilised egg there comes to be a person" and how might we also explain being the same person over time (Olson, 2023). The concept of personal identity involves accounting for socialisation, and it also consists of identifying crucial factors that account for the emergence of a human agent with distinctive psychological, cultural, and social features over time (Menkiti, 1984). Whereas the literature in the West tends to account for personal identity by appealing to individualistic properties like a soul or psychological properties like rationality, consciousness, and memory (I think therefore I am), the literature in African thought tends to place emphasis on social relationships to account for personal identity (I am because we are).

Remember, we also specified the normative concept of a person, which we described in terms of virtue. There is another distinct normative concept of a person, which we should distinguish from that of virtue. Kevin Behrens (2013) in the essay 'Two "Normative" Conceptions of Personhood' identifies two distinct normative concepts of a person: one is *agent-centred* and another is *patient-centred*. The notion of a person I have described in terms of (the acquisition of) virtue is the same as the agent-centred notion of a person. The agent-centred notion embodies values or virtues relative to the quality of the agent's actions, conduct, and character. One could be more or less of a person depending on the quality of her actions and disposition; the goal is to become more of a person. The patient-centred notion of a person is tantamount to the technical idea of moral status and/or human dignity in ethics and applied ethics (Behrens, 2013; Molefe, 2020; Molefe and Muade, 2024). The patient-centred notion of a person – moral status – is prominent in bioethical debates involving the beginning-and-end-of-life issues, amongst others (Schulman, 2008). The idea of moral status associates value with the kind of a thing the entity is, and it does so, typically, by identifying the morally salient or relevant metaphysical properties. To be described as a person in this sense indicates one bearing such a designation possesses the relevant metaphysical property, or one denied such a designation of a person lacks the relevant capacities (see Molefe and Muade, 2024).

For an example of the patient-centred notion of a person, consider the literature on the abortion debate in moral philosophy (Hursthouse, 2013). The debate on this literature pivots on whether a foetus is a person or has moral status. The debate does not dispute that a foetus is a human being. What is in dispute is whether a foetus is a person in the morally relevant sense; i.e., does it have moral status? The determination of the patient-centred notion of a person, or moral status, is a function of possessing specific metaphysical capacities. If the metaphysical capacity of consciousness, self-concept, or even rationality is definitive of moral personhood, as Mary Anne Warren (1973) argues, it would follow that a foetus lacks moral status.

For another example of the patient-centred notion of a person or moral status, consider the literature on animal ethics. The debate pivots on considering whether animals can count as persons, in the sense of the patient-centred notion of a person, or whether they have moral status, which (if they do have moral status) would secure them certain negative and positive duties, or rights designed to protect and empower them (Clarke, 1977; Hursthouse, 2013; Horsthemke, 2015). Proponents that defend the moral status of animals, for example, tend to posit the metaphysical capacity for sentience (Singer, 2009) or subject-of-an-experience as the basis for personhood (Regan, 1985). The point that emerges is that moral personhood, the patient-centred notion of a person or moral status, is a function entirely of whether the entity under consideration possesses the relevant metaphysical capacities. Note, it is the mere possession of the relevant metaphysical capacities, and not their use, which secures moral status. Hence, moral status is a function of being a particular kind of a thing, in as far as one possesses certain metaphysical capacities characteristic of that kind.

Above, we have noted four distinct concepts of a person, namely, personhood as a human being (P1), personal identity (P2), virtue (P3), and moral status (P4). We can now proceed to associate the distinct senses of personhood to the three components in the saying constitutive of Ubuntu ethics: (a) a person (b) is a person (c) through other persons. It is my view that (a) a person, embodies both the ontological (P1) and normative concept of a person (P4). We can further break (a) down into (a1) and (a2), where the former refers to the ontological notion of a human being (P1) and, at the same time, it captures the patient-centred idea of a person, or moral status (P4). When I use the concept of *umuntu*, as in the title of this chapter, I have both senses of the term in mind, with special emphasis on the moral status aspect of it. The connection between (a1) = (P1) and (a2) = (P4) is not a mysterious one given that a human being, as a matter of fact, possesses specific descriptive capacities and some of these capacities not only identify them as members of a particular ontological group, human beings, but identify ontological capacities that account for their moral importance, or moral status. The second component of the saying, (b) is a person, corresponds with the agent-centred notion of a person or *ubuntu* (P3). In this sense, to judge one to be a person, one is simply approving of the agent's actions and character as being characterised by excellence or virtue. The third component, (c) through other persons, points us to the communitarian aspect of Ubuntu ethics, which prescribes positive interpersonal or communal relations as the only context where the emergence of virtue or *ubuntu* is possible.

If my interpretation of the concepts of persons in the saying 'a person is a person through other persons' is true then it embodies the following rendition of Ubuntu as a moral perspective: (a) a human being, as the moral agent, (b) has the chief duty to become a person and (c) she can only do so in the context of positive communal relations with others. To justify my analysis and application of the concepts of a person to the saying constitutive of Ubuntu ethics 'a person is a person through other persons', I will do two tasks, one could be considered a negative argument and another a positive one.

*The Negative Argument*

There is a tendency in the literature on personhood to distinguish the ontological and normative notions of a person. In African philosophy, another tendency is to emphasise the normative notion of a person (P3) over the ontological notion of a person (P1). One encounters this tendency in the writings of some of the leading scholars of personhood in African philosophy. For example, one of the leading Nigerian African philosophers Segun Gbadegesin (1998: 194) observes that "In Yoruba language greater emphasis is placed on this normative dimension of eniyan than is perhaps placed on the [ontological] concept of person...". *Eniyan* is the word for a person in Yoruba language. *Eniyan*, Gbadegesin observes, has both the ontological and normative senses, which observation is consistent amongst African languages. He further notes that greater emphasis tends to be placed on the normative sense of personhood. If we take Gbadegesin's claim and apply it to the saying '(a) a person (b) is a person (c) through other persons', it could be interpreted to mean that (b) the normative notion of a person is more important or takes priority over (a) the ontological notion. Gbadegesin's claim would prove questionable if we note the distinction between (a1) the mere fact of being human and (a2) the value associated with the status or fact of being human (the idea of moral status), I hope this claim will be justified after reading this chapter and the next.

Another leading scholar of African thought makes a similar observation concerning the distinction between the ontological and normative notions of a person, Wiredu (2008: 13) opines "The African mind is not oblivious to the ontological aspects of the concept of a person, and has ideas thereto. But ethical issues are more dominant". Note that Wiredu's reference to ethical issues is made against or in contrast to the ontological notion of a person, the point being that the normative (moral) concept of a person is more dominant in African philosophy. The claim that the normative notion is more dominant in African philosophy can be borne out by the evidence that the literature has tended to focus on the normative concept of personhood. In this instance, when scholars refer to the normative notion of a person, they are specifically referring to the agent-centred notion of a person that points to a human agent that exudes with virtue or excellence. Wiredu (2008: 14, 16) notes that to be a called a person amounts to being "highly praised" because one is "morally sound" in as far as his/her actions demonstrate responsibility towards the self, special relationships, and the society at large.

A possible implication, which would be misleading, that can be associated with the claim that the normative notion is more dominant than the ontological one is that the value associated with what the agent does/achieves in the moral domain (b) is more important than the value associated with the value associated *umuntu* as a bearer of moral status (a2). This chapter and book aims to redress the tendency to place priority on *ubuntu* over *umuntu* by re-directing our attention to the neglected primary value associated with *umuntu* (a2). The argument that the normative notion is more important than the ontological notion is true if we are making reference to (a1) and exclude considerations associated with (a2). (a1) is a reference to the mere fact of being human that is distinct from other ontological things like trees, stones, mountains, and so on. (a2) associates certain metaphysical features of being human as the basis for their value, moral status, or human dignity.

To question the claim that the normative notion of a person is more important than the ontological one, or to suggest a more productive way to read matters concerning the ontological and normative concepts of a person, consider the example offered by Gyekye (2010) when identifying the ontological notion of a person, which we will use to make a point about the conjoined nature of (a1 = P1) and (a2 = P4). Consider a group of hunters at a game farm in Zimbabwe. They are hunting for animals. As one of them is about to shoot, his/her mates shout 'It is a person'. Without hesitating, he drops the gun and says 'I almost shot a person' with a sigh of huge relief. I argue that two things are going on here.

In the first instance, when the friends shout that 'it is a person', they are alerting their friend that he is not targeting the correct target (an animal) but a human being (a1). On the same breath, they seem to be working with a particular moral attitude or view that hunting down a human being is impermissible the way one would an animal (a2). The ontological fact of a human being (a1) is conjoined with the moral intuition or belief that there is something morally distinctive and special about being human (a2), i.e., when the shooter realises that he/she is aiming at a human being, then the moral belief about the value associated with human being kicks in accompanied by the consideration that forbids certain ways of treating human beings as bearers of moral status or value. Just by recognising that it is a person before him/her, that recognition should be sufficient to stop the hunter from shooting. The expression, 'it is a person', is at once ontological and normative. I refer to the ontological as (a1) and the normative as (a2), which indicate that certain facts about human beings serve as the basis for the value associated with them in their status as human beings. If (a2) is brought into the picture, then it problematises the tendency to regard the agent-centred notion as more important or even dominant than the ontological one. A balanced view would recognise, firstly, the place for both the ontological notion of a person (a1 and a2) and the normative notion (b) in a plausible interpretation of Ubuntu ethics; and, secondly, if we were to rank the two, (a2) and (b), in terms of priority, we would place priority on (a2) rather than (b), but the two hang together as components of a single moral theory.

*The Positive Argument*

The negative argument sought to challenge the tendency to prioritise the agent-centred notion of person over the ontological one (a2)[5]. Moreover, it also clarified that the ontological notion, the fact of being, embodies the patient-centred notion of a person, moral status, which assigns value to human beings on the basis that they possess certain value-endowing metaphysical capacities. This section proffers an argument for why we must consider the ontological notion of a person (a2), *umuntu*, to be crucial in our interpretation of Ubuntu ethics. We can distinguish *umuntu* and *ubuntu*. *Umuntu* could be understood as an ontological concept and *umuntu* matters in ethics because he/she is also a moral agent. When *umuntu* is thriving as a moral agent in Ubuntu ethics (i.e., the agent lives up to the demands of morality), his/her achievements are described in terms of *ubuntu* – we say the agent (*umuntu*) has *ubuntu*, which means her character disposition is characterised by moral excellence (Tutu, 1999; Ikuenobe, 2017). It is *umuntu* that acquires *ubuntu*, which implies the primacy and priority of *umuntu* in Ubuntu ethics in relation to *ubuntu*.

*Umuntu* is before that which is used to measure him/her as a standard of excellence (*ubuntu*). Alternatively, *ubuntu* (virtue) is not possible without *umuntu*. It is precisely the presence of *umuntu* (characterised by certain metaphysical features) that renders *ubuntu* possible in the first place. Hence, *ubuntu* requires or depends on *umuntu*, which points to the necessity of *umuntu* for the emergence of *ubuntu*.

Furthermore, if *ubuntu* represents a state of virtue (a valuable state), it is not farfetched to associate *umuntu* with a prior state of value. The argument is that it is not unreasonable to suppose that *umuntu*, in his/her own right, is a bearer of value, which is distinct and prior to that which is associated with *ubuntu*. We should take seriously this claim because it suggests that we should not only care about what *umuntu* can achieve (if she achieves it at all), but we must also care about *umuntu* before she is anything or does anything in the world. The supposition of the value associated with *umuntu* gives meaning to the value of what *umuntu* can achieve (*ubuntu*). Moreover, if *umuntu*, in his/her own right, has no value at all, what would be his/her standing morally and politically before she achieves *ubuntu* or if he/she fails to achieve it. Some basic and ineliminable value must be associated with *umuntu* for his/her moral protection before he/she can even begin the moral journey towards personhood or *ubuntu*, otherwise, the human agent would be exposed to all kinds of threats, harms, and interferences without any moral recourse if he/she is not a bearer of intrinsic value[6]. It is the supposition of the basic and ineliminable value that protects infants and the severely mentally incapacitated even though they cannot pursue the value associated with *ubuntu*. The basic value associated with *umuntu*, as he/she is, for the kind of a thing that he/she is and before she does anything in the world, would serve as a moral constraint against interferences and harms. Hence, it is reasonable to posit that *umuntu* is a bearer of intrinsic value, and moral status, which is prior and informs all other values, including the value of *ubuntu*, that the agent may go on to achieve or even fail to do so.

In this section, we noted the four distinct concepts of a person with the aim to use them to interpret the saying '(a) a person (b) is a person (c) through other persons' that constitutes the ethical vision of Ubuntu. We noted four distinct concepts of a person: (1) a human being (P1), (2) personal identity (P2), (3) virtue or excellence (P3), and (4) moral status (P4). (P1) and (P2) are ontological notions, and (P3) and (P4) are normative notions. There is a connection between (P1) and (P4). Concerning the saying 'a person (a) is a person (b) through other persons' (c), we noted that the ontological notion (P1) of 'a person' (a) can be subdivided into (a1) and (a2). (P1) *qua* (a1) captures the fact of being human, and (P1) *qua* (a2) captures the value associated with being human, which is the same as moral status, P4. Hence, (a2) = (P4). Concerning the normative notion of a person (b), we noted that it corresponds with *ubuntu* or moral excellence, which the agent must pursue and if successful, achieve or acquire. In relation to (c), we noted it prescribes the community or social relations as the only context where (b) can be negotiated and achieved.

I emphasise that in my interpretation and analysis of Ubuntu ethics, (a1) corresponds with (P1), which refers to the ontological notion of a person – the bare fact of being human. (a2) corresponds with (P4), which refers to the normative concept of a person, the *patient-centred* of a person, which is equivalent to the idea and the value of moral status that the agent has because he/she is human or bears certain metaphysical capacities. (b) corresponds with (P3), which refers to the normative notion of a person, and the *agent-centred* notion, which refers to a virtuous character disposition, or *ubuntu*.

Moreover, I argued that we should distinguish between two distinct values in two ways. Firstly, I disputed the claim that the normative notion should receive more emphasis than the ontological one, particularly if we note (a2) and/or (P4) that captures the kind of value that tracks metaphysical features of being human, the idea of moral status. Secondly, I argued that *umuntu* should be considered to possess (intrinsic) value prior to pursuing and achieving *ubuntu*, otherwise *umuntu* would be rendered morally and politically vulnerable to all kinds of harms, abuses, and interferences.

The following section explores the value associated with *umuntu*, intrinsic value and human dignity.

## *Umuntu*, Intrinsic Value and Human Dignity

This section begins by distinguishing between intrinsic and extrinsic value. It proceeds to associate *umuntu* with intrinsic value, which I will explain in terms of moral status and/or human dignity. I will further define the concept of human dignity, provide an Ubuntu-based theory, and explain three functions associated with human dignity in moral-political philosophy.

### *Intrinsic and Extrinsic Value*

In her brilliant article 'Two Distinctions of Goodness', Christine Korsgaard (1983) distinguishes between two kinds of values, intrinsic and extrinsic. 'Intrinsic value' refers to a value located inside or internal of a particular object, which has value in and of itself. The kind of value described as intrinsic ties value to certain innate features of the object under consideration. The value associated with things like beauty and pleasure, amongst others, can be considered intrinsic in that it inheres in the thing itself. The value associated with pleasure is located (or inherent) in the pleasurable experiences themselves. The same goes for beauty. Extrinsic value, on the other hand, refers to the kind of value that is external or depends on other things for its value. Money serves as the perfect example of extrinsic value. Money, in and of itself, has no value; its value depends on a variety of factors external to it. For this reason, it is often backed by some economically valuable mineral like gold or oil, and its value changes relative to the market dynamics.

This distinction is crucial as it will help us understand the values associated with *umuntu* and *ubuntu*. If the value associated with *ubuntu* is the kind that we are not born with and we have to pursue it, and, if successful, we can acquire it, then it should immediately follow that it is a kind of a value that is not intrinsic. If, however, the value associated with *umuntu* is a function of certain metaphysical features characteristic of being human, then suggests it is characterised by intrinsic value. That is, *umuntu*, or at least, the value associated with *umuntu*, is an intrinsic one, which means *umuntu* has value as he/she is. In moral philosophy, human beings, if they possess intrinsic value, then we can say, they have moral status or human dignity (Hughes, 2011; Miller, 2017). I use the ideas of moral status and human dignity interchangeably (see Toscano, 2011; Molefe and Muade, 2024)[7]. Before we proceed, we must justify the connection between *umuntu* and intrinsic value, or human dignity in light of the literature on Ubuntu ethics.

### *Umuntu as a Bearer of Human Dignity*

The aim of this discussion is to clarify the place and importance of *umuntu*, as a bearer of intrinsic value or human dignity, in African thought, which also involves clarifying the relation between *umuntu* and human dignity. The importance of *umuntu* in Ubuntu ethics is enunciated by the very saying 'a person is a person through other persons'. One could easily note two things about this saying. Firstly, it imagines a human-centred approach to morality. This is the case because from the beginning, 'a *person*', to the end, 'through other *persons*' places and mentions only humans beings in its imagination of morality (Wiredu, 1992; Gyekye, 1992, 1997). The sole and repeated mention of *umuntu* might be indicative of the importance of *umuntu* in African moral thought.

Secondly, the imagination of morality that solely refers to human beings might be criticised for being anthropocentric (Horsthemke, 2015). In this chapter, I wish to follow the first line of inquiry that focuses on the importance of *umuntu* in African ethics. (This should not be read to suggest that the criticism of anthropocentrism should not be taken seriously; a response to concerns of anthropocentrism, as important as it might be, is not the focus of this chapter.) The debate concerning anthropocentrism, weak anthropocentrism, and non-anthropocentrism is raging on in the literature on African philosophy (see Behrens, 2010, Metz, 2012; Horsthemke, 2015)[8].

There are at least two ways to make sense of the importance of human beings, *umuntu*, in Ubuntu ethics. The first way revolves around *umuntu* as a moral agent and the second considers *umuntu* as a moral patient. In terms of the argument for the importance of human beings as moral agents, one would notice the prevalent idea that human beings bear more special duties and responsibilities in the world than any other thing or being in the world. For example, note Ramose's (2009: 309, emphasis mine) remark – "Without such care, the interdependence between human beings and physical nature would be undermined. Moreover, human beings are indeed an intrinsic part of physical nature although possibly a *privileged* part". Ramose correctly locates human beings as part of the natural world and he insists that human beings must foster a culture of interdependence and harmony with all living and non-living things if the planet is to be our home and the home of all that are in it. He goes a step further, however, to also alert us that human beings are not just a natural part of the world, but they are a privileged part of it. There is a privilege associated with being a human being, which no other natural entity in the world has or enjoys.

Another leading scholar of African thought, Godfrey Tangwa (2004: 388) describes the privilege associated with being human in terms of "humankind [being] the apex of biological existence". Tangwa defends the claim that human beings are a privileged part of nature or the apex of biological existence by appealing to the asymmetry of responsibilities, which he describes in this fashion – "…while human beings have putative moral responsibilities toward inanimate objects, plants, and the 'lower' animals, these latter cannot be considered, without absurdity, as having any reciprocal moral obligations toward humans" (Tangwa, 2004: 388). Ramose expresses the prevalent belief in African moral cultures that human beings are considered to be more important in the natural world because they have more capability and responsibility towards living and non-living things than these other things can have towards human beings. The point of the argument by appealing to the lack of symmetry in terms of moral responsibilities between human beings and other things in the world is by no means to suggest that human beings are justified to interfere with other things arbitrarily or that the planet cannot survive without human beings; instead, it is to point out that only human beings can bear greater responsibility towards other things in the world. This argument suggests the importance of human beings by pointing to their greater capacity and responsibility in the natural world.

The second argument to justify the privileged status of human beings in the natural world or their status of being the apex of the biological apex is in terms of the moral patient argument, which hinges on the idea of human dignity. The concept of human dignity denotes moral worth or preciousness associated with the fact of being human, which imposes duties of respect towards moral agents (Donnelly, 2015). There is scepticism or even rejection of the idea of human dignity in the literature on moral philosophy. Some scholars consider the concept of human dignity to be useless or insist that we should jettison it altogether (Macklin, 2003; Pinker, 2008). This scepticism manifests in the literature in the Western tradition of philosophy, but it is generally absent in the African tradition of philosophy. The prevalent intuition in African philosophy tends to endorse the concept of human dignity, though the concept is generally under-theorised in African philosophy (Donnelly, 1982; Wiredu, 1992; Gyekye, 1992; Ilesanmi, 2001; Bujo, 2001).

I will, on the main, draw from the work of Mogobe Ramose on Ubuntu to explain the privileged place of human beings in the world in terms of the idea of human dignity. I do so because Ramose is arguably one of the leading scholars of Ubuntu in African philosophy. Not only is he trained as a philosopher, but he also enjoys the privilege of being an African and a cultural insider concerning the customs and values associated with the Bantu peoples that adhere to Ubuntu as a philosophy and a way of life. In my previous work, I accounted for the privileged status of human beings as bearers of intrinsic value or human dignity by drawing from the works of Menkiti and Gyekye (see Molefe, 2020, 2021, 2022). Scholars of African thought usually demonstrate the intrinsic and high value associated with the fact of being by drawing a comparison between human beings and animals and, ultimately, conclude that human beings are morally distinct, special, and superior in the moral and political spheres than other living things (Menkiti, 1984; Wiredu, 1996; Bujo, 2001; Metz, 2012; Molefe, 2020). These scholars account for the moral specialness of human beings in terms of the idea of human dignity.

Typically, scholars invoke the saying 'a person is a person through other persons' to account for Ubuntu ethics. There are other sayings in African cultures that accompany and along it shed more light on Ubuntu ethics. Ramose in his exposition of the importance of *umuntu* (or, *motho*, in seSotho language) invokes the seSotho saying *feta motho o tsware kgomo* (Ramose, 1999, 2009, 2010). Ramose (1999: 4) considers the saying '*feta motho o tsware kgomo*' "a fundamental principle of African philosophy". In another place, Ramose (2020) observes that "*Feta kgomo o Tsware motho* is the ethical dimension of ubuntu". In my view, the saying *feat kgomo o tsware motho* is fundamental or the ethical dimension of ethics since it captures the significant value associated with *umuntu, motho, or* a person (a1 and a2). According to him, "*Feta kgomo o tshware motho*—directly translated as 'go past the cow and catch the human being' is an ethical maxim in the African philosophy of Ubuntu among the Bantu-speaking peoples" (Ramose, 1999: 4).

Notice two things in the above quotation. Firstly, it provides us with a translation of the saying, which involves comparing the value of a human being (*motho/umuntu*) and that of a cow (*kgomo*). This comparison reflects the tendency to compare or contrast the value of a human being, *umuntu*, and that of an animal, a cow, *kgomo*. Secondly, Ramose is emphatic that this saying is a fundamental ethical maxim, i.e., it embodies an ethics that points us to the moral importance of *motho* (*umuntu*), or a person. The underlying moral message is that the value of a human being is greater than that of a cow. To make progress in our analysis, we may need to inquire – what does it mean to go past a cow and catch a human being? What fundamental ethical insight is inherent in this saying?

In relation to the meaning of this saying, Ramose (1999: 4) opines –

This (saying) means that if and when a choice must be made between the preservation of human life and the possession of wealth that may be dispensed with then it is imperative to choose the preservation of human life.

The saying is interpreted to present two competing values: the value of wealth and the value of human life. The distinction in terms of two values revolves around *motho* (seSotho word for *umuntu* or a person) and *kgomo* (a cow). Ramose considers the value of a human being (*umuntu*) to be distinct from that of a cow. In a situation where we have to choose between the two, supposing we are in a trade-off situation, Ramose stipulates that we ought to treasure and protect the human being over the cow. Note, a cow in the cultures of the BaSotho and the Nguni peoples, below the Sahara, represents money or wealth, it is a central currency and commodity for facilitating transactions. The saying *feta kgomo a tsware kgomo* enunciates an ethical principle that places a prime on a human being over wealth in the fashion of the distinction stipulated by Kant between worth and price – *Umuntu* embodies worth and a cow price (Kant, [1785] 1996).

In another context, Ramose (2010: 302, emphasis mine) associates the saying with human dignity as follows – "... the practice of *feta kgomo o tshware motho* ... requires the moral education based upon the principles of sharing, concern for one another and the subordination of wealth to *the dignity of the human person as motho*". According to Ramose, the saying recognises the dignity of the human person, i.e., it considers *umuntu/motho* as the bearer of the supreme value of dignity, which value far surpasses and supersedes that of wealth. To conceive of *umuntu* as a bearer of dignity denotes that he/she possesses the kind of value, worth, that is inherent, incomparable, and superlative (Hughes, 2011). Hence, we should highly prize a human being over wealth. To accentuate the connection between *umuntu* and human dignity in relation to saying *feta kgomo o tsware kgomo* note this remark by Ramose – "In this sense human dignity is crucial and decisive ... Human dignity and its decisive importance in African philosophy is ... expressed by the saying, *feta motho otsware kgomo*" (1999: 127).

Hence, in light of one the central sayings in Ubuntu ethics *feta motho o tshware kgomo*, we encounter the idea of the importance of a human being that I explain in terms of human dignity. *Umuntu* is a bearer of intrinsic value or human dignity. There are two ways to think about *umuntu* (a person) in terms of their relation to the notion of dignity. Firstly, one can understand it in terms of human beings having *intrinsic* value, or moral worth. Alternatively, as Ramose (2009: 420) states, "the individual human being is an object of *intrinsic value*". To talk of 'intrinsic value' is to appreciate human beings' moral distinctiveness and preciousness, which locates their value in certain innate features of their nature or natural endowments. To say the value associated with human beings is *intrinsic* means to emphasise that it is not derived, borrowed, or dependent on any other entity. In terms of value, each human individual is a bearer of underived and inalienable worth. Whereas the value of a cow is dependent and derives in a culture and its usefulness in that social context to measure and facilitate social and economic transactions, the worth of a human being is intrinsic and independent of the social context and its contingencies.

The idea of human dignity not only signifies intrinsic value but also the superlative *status* associated with human beings (Rosen, 2012). The high station or status associated with human beings is predicated on them being bearers of intrinsic value. Human dignity allows us to appreciate the intrinsic value of human beings, which (value) secures them their moral and political status as deserving the highest regard in the socio-political order. The status of dignity associated with human beings derives from their intrinsic value and the status of human dignity functions to protect their intrinsic value. Consider, as an example of the distinction between dignity as intrinsic value and as a status, the case of a royalty. One is royalty because of certain intrinsic biological features, such as being born of and in the royal family. One must have the intrinsic property of the royal blood to have the potential to be royalty. His/her royalty status, in part, derives from him/her having royal blood running in his/her veins. The status of royalty functions to secure her "a particular package of rights, powers, disabilities, duties, privileges, immunities, and liabilities accruing to a person by virtue of the condition or situation they are in" (Waldron, 2013: 24).

In my view and interpretation of Ubuntu ethics, human dignity is both a value-and-status term. As a value term, it points us to the intrinsic worth associated with *umuntu* as he/she is without regard to conditions in her own life, good or bad, or the world as a whole. It is a value she possesses as he/she is. This value secures her superlative status in the world, which status specifies burdens (her responsibilities and obligations towards others) and benefits (the duties, rights, and resources we owe towards him/her) associated with beings occupying such a status. I will explain the burdens and benefits associated with human dignity below in terms of the functions of human dignity.

Next, I provide a sketch of an Ubuntu-based theory of human dignity.

## Ubuntu and a Theory Human Dignity

Above, I established the view that *umuntu* is a privileged part of nature or is at the apex of biological existence, claims that express the importance of human persons, by associating him/her with intrinsic-and-status dignity. Now, I proceed to consider how Ubuntu might theoretically explain or account for the intrinsic value we associate with *umuntu*, or human dignity. This task involves specifying the value-bearing endowments of *umuntu* that constitutes his/her intrinsic value. In other words, we will account for the intrinsic value or human dignity by considering the distinctive features of our nature that render us morally precious as a species. In Western intellectual cultures, scholars tend to account for human dignity relative to us possessing particular psychological or cognitive abilities such as autonomy, a soul, basic capabilities, or the capacity for care (Singer, 2009; Nussbaum, 2011; Metz, 2012; Miller, 2017). Different theories of human dignity account for it variously relative to what property they posit as the basis for it (Jaworska and Tannenbaum, 2013). Note that the properties usually invoked to account for human dignity are some endowments of our nature, be it rationality or basic capabilities. The notion of *endowments* is crucial as it denotes that the features that account for human dignity are internal properties of our nature.

To account for an Ubuntu-based account of human dignity, we have to consider and specify the endowment of our human nature that accounts for our intrinsic value. Notice, for starters, that Menkiti (1984: 178) explains our intrinsic value in terms of the human "capacity for moral sense". The capacity for moral sense, according to Menkiti, is the most valuable aspect of our nature as human beings, which renders us distinct and special in the natural realm. For another, consider Gyekye's (1992: 110) comment concerning the agent-centred notion of a person (*ubuntu*), where he specifies "the capacity for moral sense" as the endowment that secures our intrinsic value or human dignity. Gyekye explains the capacity for moral sense to refer to a human being "being capable of moral choice, that is, having the moral sense to distinguish between good and evil or right and wrong" (Gyekye, 1992: 110). In my reading, Gyekye seems to regard the capacity for moral sense to be the same as "the capacity for virtue" (Gyekye, 1992: 10). Broadly, the capacity for virtue consists of all the psychological endowments one requires to be able to cultivate a virtuous disposition, which involves cognitive, emotional, and relational capacities. Hence, I stipulate that Ubuntu ethics accounts for human dignity in terms of the human capacity for virtue. In this light, we can conclude that as much as Kant accounts for human dignity in terms of the capacity for autonomy, Ubuntu ethics accounts for it in terms of the capacity for virtue. We note, therefore, *umuntu* is intrinsically valuable or has human dignity because he/she possesses the capacity for virtue[9].

## Umuntu and the Function of Human Dignity

We have secured the view that *umuntu* is a bearer of intrinsic value, or human dignity, which also grounds his status dignity. What is the moral and political consequence of construing *umuntu* as a bearer of intrinsic value or human dignity. Alternatively, what is the significance of associating *umuntu* with human dignity? The literature on human dignity in moral philosophy considers human dignity to be crucial and decisive because it is associated with three functions in social and political contexts: constraints, duty to aid or empowerment, and egalitarianism (see Beyleveld and Brownsword, 2001; McNaughton and Rawling, 2006). We might also consider these functions of human dignity as a way to capture the package of burdens and benefits associated with the status of human dignity, which serve to protect intrinsic value. The idea of *constraints* forbids certain ways to relate or treat a being of dignity (McNaughton and Rawling, 2006). Certain ways to relate with beings that have intrinsic value are absolutely forbidden because they harm, degrade, or even dehumanise such a being (Habermas, 2010). The idea of constraints conveys two important moral ideas.

On the one hand, in relation to the idea of intrinsic value, the idea of constraints points to the inalienable value associated with human beings, i.e., there is absolutely nothing in the world, not even the agent or his/her culture or political situation can separate her from his/her natural state of value (Hughes, 2011). On the other hand, the idea of constraints conveys the idea of inviolability, i.e., we have a stringent negative duty not to harm a being of dignity (Jaworska and Tannenbaum, 2013). In simple terms, so long as a being has inalienable value, we have an obligation not to violate it. The powerful idea behind the implications of human dignity in relation to constraints is the insight that we should not sacrifice, harm, or degrade a being of value to maximise value, i.e., we should not instrumentalise it for human beings economic, legal, or political goals (Kaufmann et al., 2011). A human being, as a bearer of dignity, deserves to be treated with utmost respect, which is politically powerful to forbid racism, xenophobia, rape, torture, and so on since they involve violating our humanity. Hence, we note that *umuntu* as a bearer of dignity has an inalienable value that is inviolable, or that should not be violated.

The second function associated with human dignity imposes duties on the state and moral agents to aid or *empower* beings of dignity. All things being equal, we have a duty to create situations or even conditions appropriate for the existence of beings of dignity (Nussbaum, 2011). Note, we must not only not harm beings of dignity, but we must (where possible) also provide conditions that will enable them to develop and exercise their capacities, abilities, and talents to ensure the possibility of a decent life. A dignified life is possible only under certain socio-political conditions. Access to enabling socio-economic resources and political conditions, such as public health, education, opportunities for meaningful employment, security, proper infrastructure, and so on, are important forms of empowerment in as far as they enable the individual "to exercise that capacity or capability" for virtue (Kittay, 2005: 101). Jaworska and Tannenbaum (2013) speak of empowerment in terms of our strong duties to aid beings of dignity. Hence, *umuntu*, as a bearer of dignity is owed by institutions and individuals strong duties to empower her to lead a dignified life. The state owes *umuntu* empowering conditions of existence, which will ensure a dignified existence.

Finally, the idea of human dignity is important because it offers us a way to conceptualise moral egalitarianism. Moral egalitarianism captures "the idea that all people have equal value" (Beltzer, 2014: 643). Egalitarianism embodies the attractive moral and political idea that everyone should count equally. It also suggests that we are all equal in our standing in our collective sharing in the status of being *umuntu*. Michael Rosen's (2012: 31) analysis of human dignity notes "that dignity and equality go together". If all human beings have dignity, and this dignity is a function of merely possessing a particular ontological capacity, in the case of Ubuntu ethics – the capacity for virtue – it should follow that we are equal. We account for equality amongst individuals, as citizens and/or moral patients, in terms of them possessing the morally relevant endowment, specifically, the capacity for virtue. The basic insight behind this way of accounting for equality is that since we all have the capacity to pursue virtue, which explains our equality, without regard to whether we ultimately succeed or fail in developing it to acquire *ubuntu*, we deserve to be treated with equality. Hence, anyone with this capacity is equal to every other with the same capacity. In this sense, the notion of human dignity explains to us why and/or how a white, black, female, homosexual, drunkard, criminal, and so on are all morally equal, merely because they possess the capacity for virtue. Hence, we need to recognise and appreciate *umuntu* as a bearer of intrinsic value, we should create moral political conditions, constraints, empowerment, and equality that render human existence decent and meaningful.

In light of the above exposition of Ubuntu, specifically the idea of umuntu and its relation to moral status, or human dignity, we can conclude that *umuntu* is intrinsically valuable, which also secures her superlative status. This human condition of intrinsic value is associated with certain benefits and burdens, which function to preserve and protect our intrinsic value. *Umuntu* must be considered to be inviolable, he/she requires empowering socio-economic and political conditions and must always be treated with equality without regard to whether he/she has or will achieve *ubuntu*. *Umuntu* is entitled to all these goods because he/she is a being of dignity, which is a function of his/her capacity for virtue.

## Conclusion

This chapter sought to account for the foundational value of Ubuntu ethics. To do so, it provided an analysis and interpretation of the saying 'a person is a person through other persons'. We divided the saying into three components centred on the idea of a person, (a) a person (b) is a person (c) through other persons. We further noted that (a) can be broken into (a1) the fact of being human and (a2) the value associated with the fact of being human, human dignity. We distinguished four distinct concepts of a person, the fact of being (P1), personal identity (P2), *ubuntu* or virtue (P3), and moral status (P4). We noted that the saying 'a person is a person through other persons' amounts to the moral view that a human being, as a moral agent, can pursue and attain moral excellence (or *ubuntu*) by positively engaging in social relationships with others. In relation to the human being, the ontological notion of a person, we observed that it should be conjoined with the patient-centred notion of person (moral status or human dignity), which captures the intrinsic value of a human being.

I further analysed the saying *feta motho o tsware kgomo* to affirm the moral significance of *umuntu* as a bearer of human dignity. I proposed an understanding that considers dignity to be both a value and status. It is a value term as it indicates our intrinsic value, which we have because we have the capacity for virtue. The intrinsic value associated with *umuntu* grounds our superlative status. The status of *umuntu* is associated with a certain package of burdens and benefits, which function precisely to protect our intrinsic value. We associated the status of human dignity with three functions, namely, constraints, empowerment, and egalitarianism, that serve as moral and political means to treasure and protect our intrinsic value. In this light, we note that *umuntu* is a primary and/or foundational value in Ubuntu ethics.

The next chapter turns to the second value associated with *ubuntu*.

## Notes

1 The words *umuntu* (Zulu) and *motho* (sotho) are equivalents of the English word person. The word person, in this context, specifically refers to a human being as a specific ontological kind as opposed to a tree or insect. I have used these three words, *umuntu*, *motho*, and person, interchangeably throughout this chapter and book unless specified otherwise.

2  In this and previous paragraph, I have associated 'a person' with the primary value, 'through other persons' with a secondary value, but I have not made any reference to or associated 'through other persons' with any value. This move is deliberate. Firstly, there is no chapter in the book dedicated to 'through other persons'. Secondly, 'through other persons' will feature in the next chapter as an instance of the relationalism, or, more accurately, moral relationalism, which prescribes certain social relationships as the only context where the emergence of 'is a person' or *ubuntu* is possible.
3  The omission of 'through other persons' is anticipated and covered by endnote 3.
4  I consider the concepts of moral status and human dignity to be interchangeable.
5  I urge the reader to keep in mind that the use of the phrase 'ontological notion' must always be understood to have both the merely descriptive dimension (a1, the mere fact of being human) and the evaluative dimension (a2, the value associated with being human). It is the latter (a2) that is the focus of the comment that disputes the priority placed on the normative notion of a person *qua* the agent-centred notion over the ontological notion *qua* moral status (the value associated with being human).
6  This argument anticipates the first function associated with human dignity of constraints, which imposes universal negative duties of non-interference or non-harm.
7  In my view, to have moral status and human dignity may be used interchangeably. The reason for this is that the idea of moral status, at least as I use it here, I understand it to admit of degrees, where some object might have less moral status and some might have high or even full moral status. The highest or full moral status is tantamount to human dignity.
8  In various places, I have indicated that Ubuntu ethics should be associated with plausible forms of anthropocentrism, in the form either of weak or enlightened anthropocentrism (Molefe, 2020).
9  Please note the crucial distinction between the *capacity for virtue* and the actual acquisition of virtue. The former refers to a distinctive human metaphysical capacity or endowment of our nature, whereas the latter refers to its proper development and its use. This distinction will be crucial in the next chapter, the focus of this chapter is on the capacity that grounds morality.

## References

Behrens, K. (2010). Exploring African Holism with Respect to the Environment. *Environmental Values* 19: 465–484.

Behrens, K. (2013). Two 'Normative' Conceptions of Personhood. *Quest: An African Journal of Philosophy* 25: 103–119.

Betzler, Monika (2014). Personal Projects and Reasons for Partiality. *Social Theory and Practice* 4, 683–692.

Beyleveld, D. and Brownsword, R. (2001). *Human Dignity in Bioethics and Biolaw*. Oxford: Oxford University Press.

Bujo, B. (2001). *Foundations of an African Ethic: Beyond the Universal Claims of Western Morality*. New York, NY: The Crossroad Publishing Company.

Clarke, S. R. L. (1977). *The Moral Status of Animals*. Oxford: Oxford University Press.

Donnelly, J. (1982). Human Rights and Human Dignity: An Analytic Critique of Non-Western Conceptions of Human Rights. *American Political Science Review* 76: 303–316.

Donnelly, J. (2015). Normative Versus Taxonomic Humanity: Varieties of Human Dignity in the Western Tradition. *Journal of Human Rights* 14: 1–22.

Gbadegesin, S. (1998). Eniyan': The Yoruba Conception of a Person. In P. H. Coetzee and A. P. J. Roux (Eds.), *Philosophy from Africa: A Text With Readings*. Johannesburg: Thomson Publishing.

Goulet, D. ([1996] 1997). Development Ethics: A New Discipline. *International Journal of Social Economics* 24: 1160–1171.

Gyekye, K. (1992) *Person and Community in African Thought. Person and Community: Ghanaian Philosophical Studies*, 1, KwasI, Wiredu and Kwame, Gyekye. Washington, DC: Council for Research in Values and Philosophy.

Gyekye, K. (1997). *Tradition and Modernity: Philosophical Reflections on the African Experience*. New York, NY: Oxford University Press.

Gyekye, K. (2010). African Ethics. In E. N. Zalta (Ed.), *The Stanford Encyclopedia of Philosophy*. Accessed 13 October 2019. https://plato.stanford.edu/entries/african-ethics.

Habermas, J. (2010). The Concept of Human Dignity and the Realistic Utopia of Human Rights. *Metaphilosophy* 4: 464–480.

Horsthemke, K. (2015). *Animals and African Ethics*. New York, NY: Palgrave Macmillan.

Hughes, G. (2011). The Concept of Dignity in the Universal Declaration of Human Rights. *Journal Religious Ethics* 39: 1–24.

Hursthouse, R. (2013). Moral Status. In *International Encyclopedia of Ethics*. Hoboken, NJ: John Wiley & Sons.

Ikuenobe, P. (2016). Good and Beautiful: A Moral-Aesthetic View of Personhood in African Communal Traditions. *Essays in Philosophy* 17: 124–163.

Ikuenobe, P. (2017). The Communal Basis for Moral Dignity: An African Perspective. *Philosophical Papers* 45: 437–469.

Ilesanmi, O. (2001). Human Rights Discourse in Modern Africa: A Comparative Religious Perspective. *Journal of Religious Ethics* 23: 293–320.

Jaworska, A. and Tannenbaum, J. (2013). The Grounds of Moral Status. In Zalta E (Ed.), *The Stanford Encyclopedia of Philosophy*. Stanford: The Metaphysics Research Lab, Center for the Study of Language and In-Formation, Stanford University. https://plato.stanford.edu/entries/grounds-moral-status/.

Kant, E. ([1785] 1996). *Groundwork of the Metaphysics of Morals*. Translated by M. Gregor. Cambridge: Cambridge University Press.

Kaufmann, P., Kuch, H., Neuhauser, C. and Webster, E. (2011). *Humiliation, Degradation and Dehumanisation: Human Dignity Violated*. New York, NY: Springer.

Kittay, Eva. 2005. Equality, Dignity and Disability. In *Perspectives on Equality: The Second Seamus Heaney Lectures*, edited by M. A. Waldron and F. Lyons, 95–122. Dublin: Liffey.

Korsgaard, C. (1983). Two Distinctions in Goodness. *Philosophical Review* 92: 169–195.

Lutz, D. (2009). African Ubuntu Philosophy and Global Management. *Journal of Business Ethics* 84: 313–328.

Macklin, R. (2003). Dignity is a Useless Concept. *BMJ* 327: 1419–1420.

McNaughton, D. and Rawling, P. (2006). Deontology. In D. Copp (Ed.), *Oxford Handbook of Ethical Theory*. Oxford: Oxford University Press, 425–458.

Menkiti, I. (1984). Person and Community in African Traditional Thought. In R. A. Wright (Ed.), *African Philosophy: An Introduction*. Lanham, MD: University Press of America, 171–181.

Metz, T. (2012). An African Theory of Moral Status: A Relational Alternative to Individualism and Holism. *Ethical Theory and Moral Practice: An International Forum* 14: 387–402.

Miller, S. (2017). Reconsidering Dignity Relationally. *Ethics Soc Welf* 11: 108–121.

Molefe, M. (2018). Personhood and (Rectification) Justice in African Thought. *Politikon* 45(3): 352–367.

Molefe, M. (2019). *An African Philosophy of Personhood, Morality and Politics*. New York, NY: Palgrave Macmillan.

Molefe, M. (2020). *An African Ethics of Personhood and Bioethics: a Reflection on Abortion and Euthanasia*. New York, NY: Palgrave Macmillan.

Molefe, M. (2021). *Partiality and Impartiality in African Philosophy*. Lanham, MD: Lexington Books.

Molefe, M. (2022). *Human Dignity in African Philosophy: A Very Short Introduction*. New York, NY: Springer.

Molefe, M. and Muade, E. (2024). *African Ethics and Death: Moral Status and Human Dignity in Ubuntu Thinking*. New York, NY: Routledge.

Murove, F. (2007). The Shona Ethic of Ukuma with Reference to the Immortality of Values. *The Mankind Quarterly* 48: 179–189.

Nkondo, G. (2007). Ubuntu as a Public Policy in South Africa: A Conceptual Framework. *International Journal of African Renaissance Studies* 2: 88–100.

Olson, (2023). "Personal Identity", *The Stanford Encyclopedia of Philosophy* (Fall 2023 Edition), Edward N. Zalta & Uri Nodelman (eds.), URL = <https://plato.stanford.edu/archives/fall2023/entries/identity-personal/>. Accessed 10 January 2024.

Pinker, S. (2008). The Stupidity of Dignity. The New Republic, 28 May. https://newrepublic.com/article/64674/the-stupidity-dignity

Ramose, M. (1999). *African Philosophy Through Ubuntu*. Harare: Mond Books.

Ramose, M. (2009). Towards Emancipative Politics in Africa. In F. Murove (Ed.), *African Ethics: An Anthology of Comparative and Applied Ethics*. Pietermaritzburg: University of KwaZulu-Natal Press.

Ramose, M. (2010). The Death of Democracy and the Resurrection of Timocracy. *Journal of Moral Education* 39: 291–303.

Ramose, M. (2020). *Motho Ke Motho Ka Batho*, an African Perspective on Popular Sovereignty and Democracy. In Leigh K. Jenco, Murad Idris and Megan C. Thomas (Eds.), *The Oxford Handbook of Comparative Political Theory*, online edn. Oxford Handbooks. London: Oxford Academic (11 December 2019).

Regan, T. (1985). The Case for Animal Rights. In P. Singer (Ed.), *Defence of Animals*. Oxford: Basil Blackwell, 13–26.

Rosen, M. (2012). *Dignity: Its History and Meaning*. Cambridge, MA: Harvard University Press.

Schulman, A. (2008). Bioethics and the Question of Human Dignity. In Edmund Pellegrino (Ed.), *The President's Council on Bioethics, Human Dignity and Bioethics: Essays Commissioned by the President's Council*. Washington, DC: President's Council on Bioethics, 2–19.

Singer, P. (2009). Speciesism and Moral Status. *Metaphilosophy* 40: 567–581.

Tangwa, G. (2004). Some African Reflections on Biomedical and Environmental Ethics. In K. Wiredu (Ed.), *Companion to African Philosophy*. Oxford: Blackwell Publishing, 387–395.
Toscano, M. (2011). Human Dignity as High Moral Status. *The Ethics Forum* 6: 4–25.
Tutu, D. (1999). *No Future Without Forgiveness*. New York, NY: Random House.
Warren, M. A. (1973). The Moral and Legal Status of Abortion. *The Monist* 57: 43–61.
Nussbaum, M. (2011). *Creating Capabilities: The Human Development Approach*. Cambridge, MA: The Belknap Press of Harvard University Press.
Waldron, J. (2013). Dignity and Rank. *Archives Europeennes de Sociologie* 48: 201–237.
Wiredu, K. (1992). Moral Foundations of an African Culture. In K. Wiredu and K. Gyekye (Eds.), *Person and Community: Ghanaian Philosophical Studies*, vol. 1. Washington, DC: The Council for Research in Values and Philosophy.
Wiredu, K. (1996). *Cultural Universals and Particulars: An African Perspective*. Indianapolis, IN: Indiana University Press.
Wiredu, K. (2008). Social Philosophy in Postcolonial Africa: Some Preliminaries Concerning Communalism and Communitarianism. *South African Journal of Philosophy* 27: 332–339.

# 2 Ubuntu Ethics, *ubuntu* and Human Dignity

## Introduction

The primary aim of this chapter is to systematically construct a perfectionist interpretation of Ubuntu ethics. The chapter will further associate the moral perfectionism characteristic of Ubuntu ethics with the concept of human dignity. Roughly, 'moral perfectionism' refers to an approach to ethics that accounts for the good in terms of the development of some facet of our human nature. In this approach, the target of morality is human nature. The moral agent's chief moral duty involves the development or perfection of his/her own nature (Wall, 2012). The previous chapter focused on the primary or foundational value in Ubuntu ethics, i.e., the inherent value of a human being (*umuntu*), which we explained in terms of moral status and/or human dignity. *Umuntu*, as he/she is, without doing or becoming anything, without regard to his/her sex, gender, religion, political affiliation, ideology, or class, has underived and inalienable value, intrinsic dignity, which grounds his/her superlative status that protects his/her intrinsic dignity via constraints, empowerment and egalitarianism.

Considering the analogy of a building that has a foundation and a superstructure, the previous chapter focused on the foundation. This chapter will focus on the superstructure of Ubuntu ethics. The logic of this approach to Ubuntu ethics, which construes it in terms of the analogy of a building, helps us to recognise and distinguish between the primary and secondary values. On this account of Ubuntu ethics, the intrinsic value associated with *umuntu* captures the primary value of human dignity. On the other hand, the value of *ubuntu* that we analogise with the superstructure captures the secondary value. The value of *ubuntu* is secondary since it depends on the primary value of human dignity inherent in *umuntu*. (If human beings were not endowed with the capacity for virtue, they would not be able to pursue/acquire *ubuntu*, and we would not have a basis to expect/require them, as moral agents, to develop it.) We may productively describe the secondary value associated with Ubuntu ethics, the value of *ubuntu*, as the final good, i.e., the kind of value we pursue for its own sake (Korsgaard, 1983). Whereas *umuntu* embodies intrinsic value, *ubuntu* indicates the final good expressed through a virtuous character disposition[1]. This chapter elucidates the final value of Ubuntu ethics, *ubuntu*.

To proceed with our aim to philosophically elucidate a perfectionist interpretation of Ubuntu ethics with a particular focus on the secondary value of *ubuntu*, this chapter will be structured as follows. Firstly, it will outline and provide reasons why Ubuntu ethics should be construed as a perfectionist moral theory. To do so, I will consider the literature on the normative concept of a person – the agent-centred notion of a person – which concept I will treat as interchangeable with *ubuntu*. Secondly, I will define the content of *ubuntu* or the agent-centred notion of a person. I will understand *ubuntu* to denote a humane moral agent, which state of virtue expresses itself via pro-social attitudes and actions. Thirdly, I will proceed to note some moral-theoretical implications related to *ubuntu* as the final good, specifically (a) moral individualism, where we will clarify the self-regarding and other-regarding aspects of *ubuntu*; (b) moral relationalism, where we will consider social relationships as the only context in which *ubuntu* can emerge; and (c) moral satisficing, where we will consider how we should regard and relate the value of perfection or self-realisation. I will suggest that the value of *ubuntu* is one that we should aim to have to satisfactory levels rather than to maximise it. Finally, I will present a fuller picture of Ubuntu ethics, where I will account for how we can represent the moral perfectionism characteristic of Ubuntu ethics in terms of human dignity.

Below, I offer an exposition of Ubuntu ethics as a perfectionist moral theory.

## Ubuntu Ethics as a Perfectionist Moral Theory

The book supposes that the saying constitutive of Ubuntu ethics, 'a person is a person through other persons', is open to a perfectionist interpretation. The previous chapter considered the first component of the Ubuntu ethics' saying (a) a person, where the focus was on *umuntu*, a person, in both the ontological (the fact of being human) and normative (the value associated with being human, human dignity) senses. We noted that the value associated with *umuntu* is intrinsic, intrinsic dignity. This chapter pivots on the second component of the saying (b) is a person, which is essentially about the moral agent *becoming a person*. I understand the requirement for the agent to become a person is the same as acquiring or achieving *ubuntu*. I understand the value associated with *ubuntu* as one that we can describe as the final good. The progression of ideas and values, in terms of chapters, is from intrinsic value (Chapter 1) to the final good (Chapter 2). Moreover, the call for the agent to pursue and acquire personhood or *ubuntu* is highly suggestive of the perfectionist moral frame. I will provide two reasons that I believe demonstrate that Ubuntu ethics, particularly as it calls for the agent to become a person or to acquire *ubuntu*, embodies a perfectionist or self-realisation approach to morality.

To demonstrate that Ubuntu ethics embodies a perfectionist approach, I will begin by providing a sample of quotations from the literature in African philosophy that endorse this kind of interpretation or that interpret the value/virtue of *ubuntu* in this fashion. Secondly, I will proceed to demonstrate the perfectionist interpretation of Ubuntu ethics by considering the ethical approach inherent in the normative concept of a person (the agent-centred notion of a person)[2].

Before I endorse the perfectionist interpretation of Ubuntu ethics, I will begin by providing a sketch of the perfectionist approach to morality. The aim is to give the reader some sense of how I understand moral perfectionism, or at least how I will use this term in this book and chapter. The literature on moral perfectionism distinguishes between *non-humanistic* and *humanistic* versions of moral perfectionism (Wall, 2012). The former approach does not associate the good with human nature. Instead, the emphasis of this approach is on the objective goods in the domains "of arts, science and culture" (cited in Wall, 2012). On the non-humanistic approach to perfectionism, the good revolves around "achievement or realisation of 'the best things in life'" (Wall, 2012.). The humanistic interpretation of morality essentially characterises ethics in terms of developing our human nature (Hurka, 1993).

In this chapter and book, I associate Ubuntu ethics with *human nature perfectionism*, which accounts for the good or excellence in terms of developing certain "natural or essential capacities" of our human nature (Dorsey, 2010: 59). That a humanistic interpretation characterises Ubuntu ethics should not come as a surprise given that, in terms of the debate whether African ethics is best construed in terms of ethical naturalism or supernaturalism, the literature tends to prefer the former (see Molefe, 2015)[3]. In fact, Gyekye (2010, emphasis mine) observes that "Humanism—the doctrine that takes *human* welfare, interests, and needs as fundamental—constitutes the foundation of African ethics". For another, consider Wiredu's assertion that "the first axiom of all Akan axiological thinking is that man or woman is the measure of all value" (Wiredu, 1996: 65). In another place, Wiredu (1992: 194) opines, "It is a human being that has value". The idea is that humanity is the source and essence of morality. In this view, the source and foundation of morality is human nature or some aspect of it[4].

Given that Ubuntu ethics grounds morality on human nature, it should follow that it embodies a human nature perfectionist approach, which is characterised by two important components. The first component involves identifying our human nature's distinctive or essential features that require development or perfection (Hurka, 1993; Wall, 2012). The second component consists of the duty imposed on the agent to realise or perfect her essential capacities. In the literature on African philosophy, the perfectionist approach to morality can also be described as the *autocentric* (van Niekerk, 2007) or the *self-realisation* (Metz, 2007) theory of value since it prescribes that the agent has to transform her *own* essential capacities to be characterised by virtue/excellence.

With this rough sketch of moral perfectionism, we proceed to provide and consider evidence in the literature of the perfectionist interpretation of Ubuntu ethics. Note, Benezet Bujo (1998: 24) states, "Acting in solidarity for the construction of the community allows himself to be brought to completion by this same community so that he can become a person truly". Consider also Dzobo's (1992: 227) comment, "… our people (African cultures) therefore conceive of human life as a force or power that continuously grows and recreates itself and so is characterised by continuous change and growth". For another, consider Augustine Shutte's (2001: 30) remark,

> The moral life is seen as a process of personal growth … Our deepest moral obligation is to become more fully human. And this means entering more and more deeply into community with others. So although the goal is personal fulfilment selfishness is excluded.

Finally, consider the comment by Munyaka and Motlhabi (2009: 63)

> It is more accurate to say that ubuntu is a person's self-realisation and manifestation as a human being. Having ubuntu, or being human, is identified with behaving according to one's human nature, and by implication, in a manner that befits a human being

All the above quotations, in one way or another, paint a picture of morality where the agent is engaging in a moral process aiming at personal growth or development. Bujo, a leading African scholar of theology and ethics, describes this process to be aiming at the completion or perfection of the agent's human nature in the context of interacting positively with others in the community. The goal of morality is for the agent to become a person truly. Dzobo, a Ghanaian philosopher, construes the goal of human existence to involve a process of moral growth and recreation, where the agent becomes better or improves in the moral journey. For Shutte, a Thomist scholar interested in African philosophy, morality involves enhancing the quality of our humanity, which he describes as community-based personal growth with the goal that we should be more human. Munyaka and Motlhabi understand the concept of *ubuntu* as involving the realisation or development of our human nature so that our conduct expresses true humanity. The picture from these quotations is that morality revolves around our human nature, and we must develop or perfect it continuously. The essence of morality revolves around the moral development of our human nature, which is characterised by the agent aiming "to become a *full* person, a *real* self, or a *genuine* human being, i.e., to exhibit virtue in a way that not everyone ends up doing" (Metz, 2010: 83, emphasis original). In these scholars' view, morality aims for a human being, as the moral agent, to acquire virtue.

Beyond these quotations from leading scholars of African ethics, the salient normative concept of personhood in African philosophy buttresses the perfectionist interpretation of Ubuntu ethics. Remember, we distinguish between the ontological and normative notions of personhood. The normative notion of a person is relevant in the exposition of Ubuntu ethics as an instance of perfectionist ethics[5]. Specifically, it is the agent-centred notion of a person that I believe embodies a perfectionist approach to morality. In fact, most commentators on the normative concept of a person appear to associate it with moral perfectionism, though this is often not their point of focus, as it is mine in this book. I rely on the idea of personhood to demonstrate moral perfectionism as a feature of Ubuntu ethics in the literature in African philosophy for two reasons.

The first reason involves my observation that the concept of personhood is probably the most influential in the literature on African philosophy. The concept of personhood has been at the heart of some of the most important debates in African philosophy. Consider, for example, the debate between radical and moderate communitarianism in African philosophy pivots on the idea of personhood (see Menkiti, 1984; Gyekye, 1997; Matolino, 2009; Oyowe, 2014, 2021; Molefe, 2019, 2021). These scholars believe that a correct conception of personhood is crucial for a plausible ethical and political system.

The second reason involves the common view in the literature that *ubuntu* and the normative concept of a person, the agent-centred one, are the same (see Metz, 2013; Ikuenobe, 2017 Molefe, 2019)[6]. In my reading of the literature, reference to an agent having *ubuntu* is the same as the judgement that some agent is a person or has achieved personhood. So much that, amongst African cultures, to declare that some human being is not a person – the denial of the status of a person to a moral agent – is the same as the denial of *ubuntu*, which judgement I understand to mean that the moral agent is living below what is expected/befits a human being (Gyekye, 1992). In my view and for purposes of this book, the phrase, (b) is a person, is equivalent (or, refers) to the idea of *ubuntu*.

In what follows, I demonstrate that the normative idea of a person embodies a perfectionist moral theory. To begin, I will draw from the works of Ifeanyi Menkiti, whose work on African personhood is amongst the most influential in the tradition of African philosophy. In fact, Wiredu (2009) claims that Menkiti was the first to offer a philosophical analysis of the concept of personhood in African philosophy. Menkiti's (1984) analysis of personhood in African philosophy distinguishes a human being as a biological organism, an ontological being of a particular kind, and the status of a person, which the agent acquires over time in the context of a robust community[7] (Oyowe, 2021). When we are born, we are merely human. We do not earn the status of being human, and it is a biological given. We cannot lose this status unless there is a fundamental change in our ontological make-up by some alien that alters our nature altogether. For Menkiti (1984: 172), the concept of a person, *umuntu*, in African cultures denotes excellence. To be recognised as a person is to associate the agent's humanity with the excellence of character.

For Menkiti, we are born human, but we have a duty to attain personhood (excellence of character or virtue). Personhood, for him, is not an event but comes in degrees in the context of a socio-moral process of transformation, where one must move from merely being human to becoming a person. Hence, Menkiti (1984: 172, emphasis mine) notes that,

> ... it is not enough to have before us the biological organism, with whatever rudimentary psychological characteristics are seen as attaching to it. We must also conceive of this organism as going through a long process of social and ritual transformation until it attains *the full complement of excellencies seen as truly definitive of man*.

Menkiti presents us with a picture of a human being that when he/she is born comes characterised by certain ontological or psychological features typical of humankind. These ontological features define us as human beings, but they are not sufficient for the status of personhood. However, when we move into the realm of morality, more is required. The goal is for a human being to be characterised by the full complements of excellence, which will mark the agent as a real, true, or genuine human being. The attainment of the status of a person, where the agent is characterised by excellence, involves the long process of socio-psycho-moral transformation. It is a process that involves the conversion of the raw endowments of our humanity to be characterised by excellence. This comment by Menkiti (1984: 173, emphasis mine) is illuminating regarding the process of transformation and its goal,

> As far as African societies are concerned, personhood is something at which individuals could fail, at which they could be competent or ineffective, better or worse. Hence, the Africans emphasised the rituals of incorporation and the overarching necessity of learning

the social rules by which the community lives, so that what was initially biologically given can come to attain social self-hood, i.e., *become a person with all the inbuilt excellencies implied by the term*.

In Menkiti's interpretation of the normative concept of a person, it involves the process of transformation where the raw features of our nature, what he describes as the biological given such as certain psychological capacities of consciousness, rationality, and so on, are transformed to be characterised by excellencies/virtues. Menkiti understands being a person, one characterised by excellence, not to be merely a cultural thing, but a deeply moral one. He refers to these as '*inbuilt* excellencies' to indicate their deep-rootedness in the agent's disposition. Deep-rootedness indicates the development and habituation of our endowments to be characterised by excellence (Gyekye, 2010). Notice also that Menkiti describes the concept of a person, and its definition, as having an "ethical sense" (Menkiti, 1984: 176). In the same passage, he describes the attainment of personhood to be associated with an agent that has achieved "ethical maturity".

In his restatement of the concept of personhood, Menkiti (2004: 326) notes that the goal of morality involves becoming "a true person, in other words, *a moral being* or bearer of norms". He further opines, "For married to the notion of person is the notion of moral arrival", which involves the acquisition or nurturing of excellence into our humanity (Menkiti, 2004). Menkiti understands personhood, the goal of morality, to involve the agent becoming a moral "saint", a "moral exemplar" in as far he/she exudes virtues (Menkiti, 2004: 326).

Consider evidence from other scholars of African thought on the normative concept of a person. Gyekye (1992: 113) opines,

> 'The evaluative statement ... 'he is a person' means, 'he has good character', he is peaceful–not troublesome', 'he is kind', 'he has respect for others', 'he is humble'. The statement 'he is a person', then, is a clearly moral statement. It is a profound appreciation of the high standards of the morality of an individual's conduct that would draw the judgment 'he is truly a person'.

In Gyekye's view, the normative or evaluative concept of a person denotes the moral agent with a good moral character. It is worth noting that Gyekye associates the agent with personhood with the high standards of morality. Thus, Gyekye associates the acquisition of personhood with the agent that has internalised and actualised the values of morality in their humanity as far as it exudes virtues.

I further draw our attention to Kwasi Wiredu's comments on the normative concept of a person. Wiredu is arguably one of the most influential

African philosophers. For Wiredu, personhood involves being morally mature, which (maturity) emerges because of developing a character disposition characterised by the social virtue of demonstrating responsibility towards oneself, special relationships, and the community at large. A person, in Wiredu's view, refers to an agent that is "morally sound" (Wiredu, 2009: 16). In his view, therefore, to be called a person is the same as being approved, praised, or commended (Wiredu, 2009: 15, emphasis mine). Wiredu (2009: 15, emphasis mine) goes further to suggest that the normative concept embodies a particular approach to morality as follows,

> How, then, do matters stand philosophically with the African idioms of normative personhood just referred to? In answering this question we begin by noting, after Kaunda, that to be called a person is to be commended. Inversely, to be called a nonperson is, in general, to be downgraded. *But such evaluation presupposes a system of values. Since the context of such evaluations is nothing short of the entire sphere of human relations, the system of values presupposed cannot be anything short of an ethic for a whole society or culture.*

The logic of Wiredu's assertion is as follows. Personhood refers to an agent that has reached a moral stature indicative of virtue or excellence. The agent achieves this status relative to the quality of his/her actions and character in his/her interactions in the community. What begins to emerge is the idea that the agent is judged against some standard of morality or excellence. Hence, to be called a person is to be commended, which indicates that the agent is doing well against some unspecified standard of evaluation. Suppose the idea of a person involves being commended. In that case, it makes sense to suppose that there must be an underlying system of values, which individuals/cultures use to apportion blame or praise to agents. Hence, Gyekye's assertion that personhood is associated with high standards of morality also presupposes a system of values. The same goes for Wiredu, who informs us that the idea of a person presupposes a system of values, and the scope of these values spans the entire sphere of human relations. Gyekye and Wiredu brilliantly lead us to the insight that the salient idea of personhood in African philosophy embodies its system of values. Unfortunately, Menkiti, Gyekye, and Wiredu do not go a step further to identify and clarify the nature of the system of values that we can associate with the idea of a person.

In this light, it becomes urgent that we clarify the nature of the system of values associated with the idea of a person in African philosophy. In a special issue dedicated to Dismas Masolo's philosophy, Kevin Behrens (2013) revisits the normative idea of a person through the philosophical writings of Menkiti, Wiredu, and Masolo, amongst others. In this analysis, Behrens makes at least two interesting observations. Firstly, he notes that the idea of a person lies at the heart of African axiological thought. The idea is that if anyone wants to comprehend African ethics, they should consider the idea of a person. Secondly, after analysing Menkiti's understanding of the concept of personhood, he comes to the following conclusion concerning the kind of ethical system it embodies,

> Menkiti's association of the term 'excellencies' with personhood also implies that becoming a person is essentially related to developing virtue. Thus, the African conception of personhood could be thought to propose a theory of ethics that brings to mind what Western philosophy calls 'perfectionism'...
> (Behrens, 2013: 111, emphasis mine)

Above, I offered some analysis of Menkiti's, Gyekye's, and Wiredu's understanding of personhood, where they tend to associate it with a character exuding excellence. Behrens correctly notices the connection Menkiti makes between personhood and excellencies: to be a person denotes a moral agent with inbuilt excellencies or a full complement of excellencies, or as Gyekye associates it with the high standard of morality. These excellencies emerge because of the community's contribution towards the agent and from the agent taking responsibility for the development of his/her own humanity so he/she may become a genuine human being (Menkiti, 1984). Behrens associates the influential concept of a person with a perfectionist system of values. Moral perfectionism is the ethical view that interprets morality to involve the agent perfecting some aspect of her human nature. In the case of Ubuntu ethics, the agent is required to develop virtue or excellencies or to have *ubuntu*. Metz also affirms Behrens' association of personhood in African philosophy with a perfectionist or self-realisation approach to morality.

In his ground-breaking article 'Toward an African Moral Theory', Metz (2007) identifies six ethical norms that tend to inform African normative theorisation, namely, life (dignity), well-being, rights, personhood (self-realisation), survival, and community. He associates these norms with six interpretations of Ubuntu ethics. His comment about the concept of personhood, as an interpretation of Ubuntu ethics, is worth noting, "This is probably the dominant interpretation of African ethics in the literature. Many thinkers take the maxim 'a person is a person through other persons' to be a call for an agent to develop her personhood", which for Metz involves "the realisation of one's distinctively human and valuable nature" (Metz, 2007: 332). The self-realisation or perfectionist approach makes the distinctive and valuable features of our human nature the target of morality, and the goal of morality involves developing or perfecting them so we may become persons or have *ubuntu*.

Until now, I have used the terms perfection and self-realisation interchangeably. At this point, it might be helpful to clarify why I insist on using the label self-realisation and perfectionism interchangeably, rather than merely using one. The underlying reason is that we might distinguish between *non-egoistic* and *egoistic* versions of moral perfectionism (Wall, 2012). Note this comment about egoistic versions of moral perfectionism,

> These theories direct each human being to perfect himself as much as possible, or at least to some threshold level. Egoistic forms of perfectionism need not be narrowly self-interested. A number of perfectionist writers have held that the good of others contributes substantially to one's own good.
>
> (Wall, 2012)

Note the comment about the non-egoistic version of moral perfectionism,

> They hold that each human being has a non-derivative duty to perfect others as well as a duty to perfect himself. Such views, at least in principle, can direct human beings to sacrifice their own perfection for the sake of others.
>
> (Wall, 2012)

The major difference between the egoistic and the non-egoistic interpretations of moral perfectionism is that the former does not impose the duty on the agent to perfect another, whilst the latter does. The former merely requires the agent to assist, empower, or create conditions, so far as is possible, that would enable another to pursue their perfection. The responsibility to pursue and attain perfection is entirely left in the hands of the agent. In comparison, the non-egoistic interpretation imposes a non-derivative duty on the agent to perfect others alongside her own duty to perfect him/herself.

Ubuntu ethics fits the egoistic version of moral perfection, where the agent has a chief duty to perfect him/herself whilst also having a duty to assist others in their quest to perfect oneself. Ubuntu ethics is described as a *self-realisation* view because it imposes the duty on the agent to transform her nature to be characterised by excellence. Ultimately, the agent either succeeds or fails in the project to perfect oneself. Moreover, the requirement to contribute to others' goal of their own perfection is reasonable and doable, but the requirement to perfect others is *too* demanding given that we have no access to crucial agential features necessary to pursue and achieve others' perfection (Molefe, 2019). By agential features, in this instance, I have in mind important psychological capacities and activities such as cognition, conation, and volition, which are essential for moral functioning (Molefe, 2019). These agential features are entirely within the locus of control of each agent; hence, the duty for moral perfection should rightly be left in each agent's domain. Our lack of access and control of another's agential features explain why we "cannot directly bring about the perfection of others" (Wall, 2012: n.p.).

In this light, it is best to understand Ubuntu ethics in terms of the egoistic interpretation of moral perfectionism. When I describe Ubuntu ethics as a *self-realisation* approach to morality, it is the egoistic version of moral perfectionism that I have in mind, which urges each moral agent to pursue their own moral perfectionism. They should, however, do so without abandoning the opportunities to assist others, as much as they too require others' assistance in their quest towards *ubuntu*[8].

Above, I provided two sets of evidence that bolster the view that Ubuntu ethics is open to a perfectionist interpretation. I began by giving a sample of quotations from some of the leading scholars of African moral thought, who, in one way or another, interpreted African morality to involve the moral development or completion of our human nature for us, as human beings, as moral agents, to become persons truly. I also considered the normative concept of a person equivalent to the final good of *ubuntu*, which I argued embodies a perfectionist system of value. Moreover, we went a step further to clarify that Ubuntu ethics embodies an egoistic version of moral perfectionism, which we capture in the literature on Ubuntu ethics and in this book as a self-realisation interpretation theory of value.

We proceed to consider the content of *ubuntu* or personhood as the final good.

## The Content of *ubuntu* as Value/Virtue

This section considers the question of the meaning of *ubuntu* as a moral term. In other words, what do we mean when we say someone has *ubuntu* or is a person? In the previous chapter, we focused on the intrinsic good, which we associated with *umuntu* as the bearer of human dignity. This chapter focuses on *ubuntu*, specifically as the goal of morality, which we can describe as the final good. In more explicit terms, Ubuntu ethics prescribes *ubuntu*, virtue or excellence, as the final good of morality. To begin, the literature defines the term *ubuntu* to denote a "Good moral disposition" (Colenso, 1861: 354), "Good moral nature" or "good disposition" (Nyembezi, 1963: 47), and "The characteristic of being truly human" (Pauw, 1975: 117). The consensus in the literature tends to define *ubuntu* in terms of *humaneness* (DeVries, 1966: 121; Samkange, 1975: 96; Biko, 1979: 214; Ramose, 2002: 75; Murove, 2014: 37; Etieyibo, 2017: 141). For example, Felix Murove's (2014: 37) remarks that "Ubuntu means humaneness – treating other people with kindness, compassion, respect and care. These virtues are usually referred to as the summation of *humaneness*".

To contextualise and understand *ubuntu* defined in terms of humaneness, we must note two crucial considerations. Firstly, notice that scholars of Ubuntu ethics associate *ubuntu* with a feature of our human nature (that feature that needs to be developed or perfected for *ubuntu* to emerge). They usually describe *ubuntu* as an innate or internal quality, which they consider to be the core of our humanity and morality. Munyaka and Motlhabi (2009: 64), for example, describe that having *ubuntu* essentially involves developing the "most important quality" of our human nature. They consider *ubuntu* to be a "positive quality" of our nature "that can fluctuate from the lowest to the highest level during one's lifetime" depending on the agent's conduct towards others (Mokgoro, 1998: 2; Munyaka and Motlhabi, 2009: 64).

I propose that we distinguish the internal capacity of our nature and *ubuntu*. The internal capacity (what we have described in our definition of perfectionist ethics as the essential capacity of our nature) refers to the raw capacity that needs to be developed. When the development is successful, *ubuntu* emerges. Here, we are drawing a distinction between two distinct qualities, one associated with our nature, the essential capacity, and another related to the development of the essential capacity of our nature. The former refers to what we described in the previous chapter as the capacity for virtue. The capacity for virtue captures our intrinsic value or human dignity. The development of our nature, the capacity for virtue, amounts to the emergence of *ubuntu*, which denotes being humane (Gade, 2011).

Secondly, above, we defined *ubuntu* as being humane, or having a humane disposition. Scholars tend to associate *ubuntu*, or being humane, with a cluster of virtues. Remember, Murove describes humaneness as a summation of a cluster of virtues. These are some of the virtues associated with *ubuntu*, or being humane. Consider, for example, Desmond Tutu (1999: 31), famous for Chairing the South African Truth and Reconciliation Commission, captures the humaneness associated with *ubuntu* as follows,

> When we want to give high praise to someone we say, 'Yu, u nobuntu'; 'Hey, so-and-so has ubuntu.' Then you are generous, are hospitable, you are friendly and caring and compassionate. You share what you have.

Some scholars associate humaneness with "kindness" (Rodegem, 1967: 129; Mayer, 1980: 70; Etieyibo, 2017: 142). In one of the most erudite expositions on Ubuntu ethics, Munyaka and Motlhabi (2009: 67) describe the individual with *ubuntu* in terms of the development of "a disposition which motivates, challenges ... one ... [to] act in humane ways towards others". They proceed to associate being humane in terms of the following virtues – "mutuality" (65), "sympathy" (71), "kindness, compassion, caring, sharing, solidarity and sacrifice" (74), "tolerance and benevolence" (75), and "openness and friendliness" (76), amongst others. Gyekye (1992: 112) defines *ubuntu*, or personhood, to involve "... moral virtues that can be said to include generosity, kindness, compassion, benevolence, respect and concern for others; in fine, any action or behaviour that conduces to the promotion of the welfare of others".

Considering the above quotations on *ubuntu* and the list of virtues they associate with having it, we can conclude that the content of *ubuntu* is captured by a humane disposition, which character disposition tends to express itself via social, relational, and/or other-regarding virtues. The virtues associated with being humane can be described as social or relational precisely because they are possible only in a context where there is social contact or interaction with another person. These are not the kinds of virtues one can have all alone, their development and exercise necessarily require a social context of positive engagement or interaction with others. Politeness, generosity, kindness, love, or any of the virtues associated with *ubuntu*, have another person, the moral patient, as their target. Hence, relational virtues' characteristic of humaneness has an essentially other-regarding component, where the moral patient is the target of the agent's moral actions. To judge some moral agent to have *ubuntu*, we are commending him/her for being humane or for having developed such a disposition, which disposition displays itself by the exercise of social virtues that benefit others. Hence, to have *ubuntu* or to be a person involves being recognised, affirmed, and praised for having a character disposition that regards, relates, and treats human beings (and possibly other sentient beings) with kindness and respect.

Above, we defined the concept of *ubuntu* to essentially refer to a virtuous or humane disposition. A humane disposition expresses itself via social or relational virtues, or other-regarding duties. We draw a distinction between two qualities in Ubuntu ethics. The first quality is a function of our nature, the essential capacity, which we have referred to as the capacity for virtue – human dignity. The second quality is a function of developing the essential capacity, the capacity for virtue, which leads to the emergence of *ubuntu*. In Ubuntu ethics, there is a sense of morality that is capacity-based, which captures moral status and/or human dignity. There is also a sense that is action-and-character-based, which refers to the virtue of *ubuntu*.

Next, we consider essential moral-theoretical elements that will help us to have a clearer and firmer grasp of Ubuntu ethics concerning the nature of the final good of *ubuntu*. Specifically, I will consider the following elements: moral individualism, moral relationalism, and moral satisficing as they relate to *ubuntu*. I begin by discussing moral individualism.

## Moral Individualism

To present the content of *ubuntu*, as the final good, in terms of humaneness, which expresses itself via other-regarding attitudes and behaviours, seems to contradict the very logic of a self-realisation theory of value, which I have indicated has a strong egoistic element. A self-realising moral theory essentially defines and connects the good with the humanity of the moral agent, where, ultimately, the agent's focus is the development of his/her human nature, some version of moral egoism. If humaneness is essentially other-regarding in its function and orientation, then it might appear misleading to represent Ubuntu ethics as a self-realising/perfectionist moral theory. Alternatively, there seems to be a tension between describing *ubuntu* as egoistic and at the same time characterising the virtues associated with it as pro-social or other regarding in their nature.

To better appreciate the tension between representing *ubuntu* as being humane, which disposition embodies relational virtues, whereas the self-realisation account tends to be agent-centred, consider Metz's (2007: 332) objection against Ubuntu ethics construed as self-realisation theory of value because it fails to accommodate an important other-regarding element of morality,

> I now question the theory's ability to provide an attractive explanation of them. If I ask why I should help others, for example, this theory says that the basic justificatory reason to do so (though not my proper motive for doing so) is that it will help me by making me more of a *mensch* or a better person. However, a better fundamental explanation of why I ought to help others appeals not to the fact that it would be good for me, or at least not merely to this fact, but to the fact that it would (likely) be good for them, an explanation that a self-realisation ethic by definition cannot invoke.

The objection against the self-realisation interpretation of Ubuntu ethics revolves around the problem occasioned for it by altruism. Altruism is essentially about the good we do for another, and the motivation and justification for such an act is another's situation of need. The objection indicates that the self-realisation theory does not provide a good explanation for why we should help another person. The objection is that the self-realisation account is implausible because it places the self, the moral agent that helps in this instance, as the basic justificatory explanation for assisting another person. In Metz's view, a morally plausible explanation ought, at least to some extent, to have the moral patient as part of the reason why the help is meted out. The egoistic element of the self-realisation theory of value renders the self the very prominent object of all moral actions. Metz's intuition and view is that there is something morally implausible about doing good for others, whilst when we do so, we only have ourselves and our good in mind. That is, the primary reason why my friend should visit me at the hospital should not be him/her feeling bad about not visiting me in my moment of distress. The reason for visiting should essentially involve that such a gesture is part of what it means to be a good friend: to show support, care, and solidarity to a friend in distress.

Remember, I am raising this objection to reveal the tension between my account of what it means to have *ubuntu*, as being humane, and interpreting Ubuntu ethics as self-realising ethics. I think the tension dissolves when we revisit the saying constitutive of Ubuntu ethics 'a person is a person through other persons'. The underlying moral logic behind this saying is the moral insight that the agent's good is not divorced from the good of others or moral patients (Lutz, 2009). The moral insight is that as a human being, the self, a moral agent must realise or perfect his/her human nature to become a real person (to have *ubuntu* or to be humane) by positively relating with others. In other words, the actions that at once help others (altruism) simultaneously empower me to become a person, i.e., "I cannot separate my humanity from the humanity of those around me" (Mbigi, 2005: 69).

The life of a moral agent in relation to others, moral patients, can be analogised with a coin – the good of the two is intertwined as the different parts of the same moral coin. Shutte (2001: 24) also opines that the context of the acquisition of *ubuntu* is a relational one, "I only become fully human to the extent that I am included in relationships with others". Ubuntu ethics imagines a relational and reciprocal morality, where the agent's actions to promote the common goals and the pursuit of the common good are not opposed to the agent's own good of personal development. In fact, the social context of interacting with others provides means and opportunities for personal growth or development, all things being equal.

The above adumbrations concerning Ubuntu ethics recognise that the agent's good (of perfecting oneself) and other-regarding duties towards others (moral patients) should not lead us to overlook the crucial aspect of moral individualism. We can note the following considerations related to what I describe as moral individualism. We can distinguish moral approaches that place a prime on some features of an individual as the focus of morality, which I describe as *moral individualism,* from those that put it on social or communitarian considerations, which I describe in terms of *moral relationalism* (May, 2014; Molefe, 2019). Ubuntu ethics marries both facets, but in this section, given my interest to clarify *ubuntu*, I will focus, mainly on the individualistic features – the next section will consider moral relationalism. Below, I identify the individualistic features of *ubuntu*.

Firstly, there is no denying that *ubuntu* has an essential other-regarding feature, where humaneness embraces and expresses itself via pro-social attitudes and actions meant to empower others. Secondly, a careful analysis of Ubuntu ethics would also appreciate the need to take cognisance of its under-emphasised self-regarding component, which lies at the heart of its *self-realisation* core – the egoistic element that imposes the duty on each agent to perfect their humanity. The focus of Ubuntu ethics is the agent's own humanity, the raw capacity, or the distinctive feature of her/his humanity, the capacity for virtue. The agent has to perfect her/his capacity for virtue, a duty that involves nurturing the capacity for virtue, which leads to the development of *ubuntu*. Hence, as far as the focus and goal of morality revolves around each agent's capacity for virtue, Ubuntu ethics has an essential self-regarding aspect.

Moreover, it is worth noting that ultimately, it is the agent, as an individual, and, in recognition, in part, of her efforts, that nurtures and attains personhood or *ubuntu*. There is no denying that the community does provide the agent, in the process of the pursuit of *ubuntu*, with crucial structural and personal resources, be it in the form of moral education or in any other way designed to enable or empower him/her. Menkiti's (1984: 172) comment on the role of the community to empower the agent in the pursuit of *ubuntu* is informative, "And during this long process of attainment, the community plays a vital role as catalyst and as prescriber of norms". Menkiti identifies at least two roles the community plays in empowering and supporting the agent in his/her quest to acquire *ubuntu*.

Firstly, the community serves as a catalyst in the agent's pursuit of *ubuntu*. The analogy of a catalyst is a useful and a powerful one. In a chemical context, a catalyst serves merely as an enabler or accelerator towards the desired or intended chemical output. In the same way, the community plays a crucial role by providing resources and opportunities that would enable the agent to acquire *ubuntu*. Secondly, the community also serves as the bearer of the standards of excellence. In the agent's journey towards moral excellence, the community provides instructions, admonitions, and exemplars to motivate and guide the agent in her quest for moral perfection. However, as much as the community plays a crucial role in empowering and guiding the agent towards the acquisition of *ubuntu*, the agent, as an individual, ought to pursue and attain *it*. When we declare some agent to have attained *ubuntu*, we are making a positive evaluation of his/her actions and character disposition, it amounts to recognising and praising him/her as an individual, for acquiring a humane disposition. Hence, we can note that Ubuntu ethics, properly construed, has both the self-regarding dimension, which involves the development of the capacity for virtue, and it also has the other-regarding component, which consists in recognising the social context of living and sharing with others in the community as the only context where the agent can learn, practice, develop, and exercise *ubuntu*.

Scholars have insisted on the communitarian aspects of Ubuntu ethics, but this section has also brought out the individualistic elements associated with it. Often, scholars tend to associate Ubuntu ethics, or the agent with *ubuntu*, with communitarian consideration like the exercise of relational virtues to the point of overlooking the individualistic features of Ubuntu ethics (Molefe, 2020). In this book and chapter, I have highlighted two individualistic features of Ubuntu ethics. Firstly, the foundation of Ubuntu ethics is the supreme value associated or inherent in the individual, the inalienable value and superlative status of human dignity. *Umuntu* is an embodiment or bearer of intrinsic value, which value is underived and unborrowed. The community does not *create* this value, instead it discovers it, and it must understand itself to have a duty to provide propitious conditions for its development and emergence (Gyekye, 1992; Murove, 2014). Notice that we as human beings, have dignity because we possess the ontological capacity for virtue. The capacity for virtue is a feature of the individual as he/she is in her own right without regard to the community. It is the individual feature of a human being, the capacity for virtue, which renders her morally precious and special and deserving of the utmost moral regard. The respect associated with human dignity is owed to each individual, in his/her own right, in virtue of him/her possessing the capacity for virtue.

The second individualistic feature of Ubuntu ethics is related to the capacity for virtue, which secures each individual human dignity. In this instance, however, the focus is on relation to the positive development and exercise of the capacity for virtue (Ikuenobe, 2017). When we declare some moral agent to have acquired *ubuntu*, we recognise and praise him/her for relating positively with his/her own capacity for virtue by developing or perfecting it. The spotlight is on the individual as a moral *agent*, specifically on how he/she could 'decorate' it with a full complement of excellencies, as Menkiti would describe it.

In summary, that which is to be the target of perfection belongs to the individual human being and ultimately, it is the individual, in his/her own right, that acquires *ubuntu*, and when we heap praises on him/her, it is in recognition of his/her own efforts and attainments (Molefe, 2017). Hence, the intrinsic value associated with *umuntu* and the acquisition of *ubuntu* captures the moral individualism characteristic of Ubuntu ethics, which is not often emphasised in the literature on African ethics.

## Moral Relationalism

The saying characteristic of Ubuntu ethics 'a person is a person through other persons' has three components: (a) a person, which refers to the ontological fact of being human and intrinsic value associated with being human; (b) is a person, the agent-centred notion of person, to have *ubuntu* or to have a humane disposition; and (c) through other persons, which prescribes the social or relational context as necessary for the emergence of *ubuntu*. On Ubuntu ethics, morality is impossible without and outside of social relationships. Notice the following comments from scholars of Ubuntu ethics commenting on its relational or communitarian aspect. For starters, notice that Menkiti (2004: 324) makes the entrance to his exposition of the normative concept of a person by appealing to the saying 'I am because we are', and he interprets it to refer to "an individual, who recognises the sources of his or her own humanity, and so realises, with internal assurance, that in the absence of others, no grounds exist for a claim regarding the individual's own standing as a person". Menkiti understands the emergence of a self as a subject and an agent to require the presence of others, or the community of human beings. He proceeds to conclude that such a relational conception of personhood should be understood to embody an approach to "morality [that] demands a point of view best described as one of beingness-with-others" (Menkiti, 2004: 324).

Consider Munyaka and Motlhabi's (2009: 68) remark,

The value and dignity of persons is best realised in relationships with others. One cannot be a human being alone, only in community. An African individual is a communal being, inseparable from and incomplete without others.

For another example of the communitarian aspect of Ubuntu ethics, consider these comments by Metz in his exposition of Ubuntu ethics. He begins by interpreting the saying 'a person is a person through other persons' to indicate that "the only way to develop moral personhood, to become a virtuous agent or lead a genuine human life is to interact with others in a certain way" (Metz, 2009: 340). In the same passage, he avers, "African ethics imply that morality is possible only through interaction with others... Morality, from a resolutely African perspective, arises only from relationships" (Metz, 2009: 340).

The point behind all these scholars' assertions is the affirmation of the centrality of interpersonal relationships and social interactions as the only viable context where morality is possible. The phrase 'through other persons' brings to the fore the importance of 'beingness-with-others' as the necessary ground to learn and practice morality. The reason for this is not far to seek. If the aim of morality involves the development of a humane disposition that manifests itself via pro-social attitudes such as care, kindness, forgiveness, tolerance, and so on, what better place can one learn and practice such social virtues other than in interpersonal relationships? If at the heart of *ubuntu* is the acquisition of a humane disposition that requires us to be kind towards others, then it should follow that interaction with others becomes the only place to learn and acquire such virtues of kindness and so on.

Scholars of African thought go further to give us a sense of how they conceive of moral relationalism. Besides stating that Ubuntu ethics requires community or positive relations with others, scholars tend to specify *harmony* as the defining feature of the relations anticipated and required by Ubuntu ethics. Tutu (1999: 35, emphasis original) opines, "Social harmony is for us the *summum bonum*—the greatest good". For another, consider Godfrey Onah's (2013: n.p.) remark, "To protect and nurture their lives, all human beings are inserted within a given community … Living harmoniously within a community is therefore a moral obligation ordained by God for the promotion of life". The essence of what lies at the heart of 'through other persons' is living harmoniously with others. Any action and character disposition that connects and enhances human relations and our humanity counts as harmony.

Surely not all forms of human connection count as harmony as anticipated in Ubuntu ethics. There are good and bad forms of community or even interpersonal relationships. For example, gangsters are a community of criminals. They connect amongst themselves as criminals, but their aims and actions tend towards harming and undermining other human beings. The kind of connection anticipated in 'through other persons' is one that has an essential component of nurturing and protecting life. Often, African scholars analogise this relationship with a wholesome family (Shutte, 2001; Behrens, 2010). Behrens (2010: ii) construes harmony to be comparable to "… family like relationships … These relationships are characterised by solidarity, shared identity and the promotion of the well-being of one another". Or as Metz, in his interpretation of harmony, argues that it has, amongst others, the essential component of good-will, where the agent demonstrates care or empowers others (moral patients) for their own sake (Metz, 2022).

In sum, moral relationalism is the idea that moral perfection, *ubuntu*, is realisable only in the context of positive relations with others. By positive relations, we mean living harmoniously, which involves connecting with others in ways that are characterised by the good-will geared towards empowering them to become better human beings in continuing relationships.

Next, I consider how to relate to the value *ubuntu*.

## Moral Satisficing

This section considers the question of how we ought to regard and relate to the value of *ubuntu*. In the literature in moral philosophy, scholars identify at least three distinct ways to relate to a value. Some approaches to morality require that we *promote* a value, others require that we *honour* it, and others prescribe that we merely *satisfice* it (Slote and Pettit, 1984; Slote, 1989; McNaughton and Rawling, 1992; Byron, 2004). The question before us involves determining whether Ubuntu ethics requires us to promote, honour, or satisfice the value of *ubuntu*. I will suggest that Ubuntu ethics requires us to satisfice the value of *ubuntu*. Before I provide reasons for this interpretation of Ubuntu ethics, I begin by providing a sketch of these three ways to relate to the value of *ubuntu*.

Some accounts of morality, like consequentialist theories, tend to prescribe that we should promote a value. Promoting a value involves maximising it, i.e., ensuring that there is as much of it in the world as possible (McNaughton and Rawling, 1992). The goal is to select those options or state of affairs that optimise the value under consideration (Slote and Pettit, 1984). In the context where we are promoting a value, the world is better off with as much of the desirable value as possible. The defining feature of promoting a value is that such an approach is compatible with instances of violating the value that is being promoted particularly if such a violation will lead to there being more of it (McNaughton and Rawling, 1992). Consider the value of honesty. If my goal involves maximising it, then if cheating on my partner once would maximise honesty in our relationship, then I should cheat, an instance of dishonesty, to optimise honesty.

Some accounts of morality, like some versions of deontological accounts, require us to recognise and respect the single instance of a value (without regard to the consequences). Consider the case of honouring the value of honesty. Respect this value would involve me being honest towards my partner and relationship even when doing so would lead her to cheat on me. My duty, on the deontological approach, involves essentially dutifully being honest to my partner without undue regard to consequences. My goal is to align my actions and character to be consistent with the value of honesty. In this approach to relating to a value, the devotion to a single instance of the value counts for its own sake.

Satisficing approaches to morality are associated with the idea of moderation, doing enough or satisfactory. The point here is that we should not always choose the best or worship values or rules for their own sake, but we should be satisfied with moderate or satisfactory levels of the value in question (Byron, 2004). If the blood-thirsty criminal comes brandishing a sword and threatening to kill my mother, I may be justified to lie about her whereabouts to protect and save her life. This is consistent with the approach to morality associated with a satisficing moral logic. Approaches that require us to maximise a value would require us to elect an action that would maximise the value. Those approaches that require us to honour a value would insist on truth-telling. Central to these three approaches to morality is the idea of the limits of morality, i.e., the scope of the demands that morality can make on us.

Intuitively, it does not seem Ubuntu ethics would require us to either promote or honour a value. Concerning how to relate to the value of *ubuntu*, Metz (2007: 332, emphasis mine) objects to a self-realising theory interpretation of Ubuntu ethics that requires us to promote *ubuntu* in this fashion,

> I submit that its fundamental emphasis on self-realisation has counter-intuitive implications. Suppose that you need a new kidney to survive and that no one will give one to you. Then, *to maximise your self-realisation*, you would need to kill another innocent person so as to acquire his organs.

The objection is misguided at two levels. Firstly, Ubuntu ethics would forbid the killing of another person for the sake of maximising self-realisation because that violates another person's human dignity (Ikuenobe, 2017). Remember, human dignity serves as a constraint against treating another human being as a means. Secondly, killing another person to maximise self-realisation is not exactly relating positively with another person. 'Through other persons' imagines participatory, transparent, and sharing relations, and murder is not part of such positive relations that enhance community and social harmony (Tutu, 1999; van Niekerk, 2007). In other words, the positive relations essential in Ubuntu ethics serve as a constraint against the maximising value associated with consequentialist ethical theories. A plausible instance of moral perfection, *ubuntu*, is one that recognises human dignity and fosters interdependence, solidarity, and community. A non-maximising interpretation of Ubuntu ethics should be preferable given its commitment to human dignity and robust social relationships characterised by good-will and care towards others.

Moreover, it seems the kind of perfectionism associated with Ubuntu ethics would not be one that value rules and/or values in an absolute fashion. For example, Ubuntu ethics would permit an agent to lie to protect a vulnerable member of the community from a blood-thirsty gang member. In fact, such an instance of deceiving the blood-thirsty gang member may be an instance of *ubuntu*. The lie is not so fundamental as to harm the dignity of the blood-thirsty gang member. Telling the truth to the gang member, however, may lead to unnecessary murder of a being of dignity. Moreover, as much social relationships are crucial in Ubuntu ethics, it does not follow that we must express positive values of such relationships towards individuals whose actions tend towards destroying the sense of community. In instances of self-and-other defence, *ubuntu* might manifest through negative means of lying or even killing the aggressor to protect another human being (Metz, 2010). This is the case because the aim is not to maximise or honour a value, but rather to manifest satisfactory levels of it consistent with the requirement to recognise human dignity and contribute towards building robust social relationships. Hence, I prefer an interpretation of Ubuntu ethics that merely require agents to satisfice the value of *ubuntu*.

The final section elucidates on Ubuntu ethics by marrying the component of *umuntu* and its attended value of human dignity with the value of *ubuntu*.

## The Final Good (*ubuntu*) and Human Dignity

In my interpretation of Ubuntu ethics, I have identified two crucial values, the values of human dignity and *ubuntu*. What I have not done this far is to explicitly explore the relationship between the two, I have merely stated that they hang together in a single perfectionist moral system. In this section, I propose one powerful way that explains how these two might hang together as part of a single ethical approach. I propose a dignity-based interpretation of moral perfectionism. I begin by drawing on important distinctions in the literature on human dignity. Scholars distinguish at least two ways we can associate dignity with a human being. We can associate dignity with a human being as a moral patient and agent. The dignity related to us merely because we are human beings is variously described as intrinsic, inherent, or status dignity (Sulmasy, 2008; Hughes, 2011; Rosen, 2012; Michael, 2014). The dignity that tracks us or emerges relative to our agency is variously described as achievement and/or inflorescent dignity (Sulmasy, 2008; Hughes, 2011; Michael, 2014).

The connection between two forms of dignity is expressed appositely by Daniel Sulmasy (2008: 473),

> By inflorescent dignity, I mean the way people use the word to describe the value of a process that is conducive to human excellence or the value of a state of affairs by which an individual expresses human excellence. In other words, inflorescent dignity refers to individuals who are flourishing as human beings—living lives consistent with and expressive of the intrinsic dignity of the human. Thus, dignity is sometimes used to refer to a state of virtue—a state of affairs in which a human being habitually acts in ways that expresses the intrinsic value of the human.

There is a kind of dignity we have merely because we are human. Sulmasy refers to this kind of dignity as intrinsic dignity. It is a dignity we have because we are the kinds of things we are, metaphysically speaking. Specifically, in Ubuntu ethics, we are the kind of thing that is essentially characterised by the capacity for virtue. This capacity for virtue renders us morally valuable. When, however, we go on to develop this capacity of our nature, we have what Sulmasy refers to as inflorescent dignity. Notice, Sulmasy associates inflorescent dignity with *human excellence, a flourishing* human being or a human being characterised by *a state of virtue*, or what in Ubuntu ethics we describe in terms of *ubuntu*.

In this light, we can interpret the moral perfectionism associated with Ubuntu ethics in terms of human dignity. We can associate *umuntu* with intrinsic dignity, as we did in Chapter 1. The kind of dignity we are born with, that is underived, inalienable, and assigns us a superlative status associated with constraints against others degrading us, requires that we are aided or empowered as agents and demands a moral-political context characterised by social egalitarianism. *Umuntu* has an intrinsic dignity because he/she has the capacity for virtue. We can also associate the acquisition of *ubuntu* with achievement or inflorescent dignity. Ubuntu ethics identifies a human being as a moral patient and agent. As a moral patient, he/she is a bearer of intrinsic dignity and, as a moral agent, if he/she does well in terms of developing her capacity for virtue, then he/she acquires *ubuntu*, or achievement dignity.

Moreover, we can proceed to note that there are two kinds of ways we are required to respond to intrinsic and achievement dignity. We can think of the way to respond to beings of dignity in terms of appropriate moral recognition, which we describe in terms of respect. Stephen Darwall's distinction between *recognition* and *appraisal* respect fits perfectly into a perfectionist scheme that distinguishes between intrinsic and achievement dignity. The recognition that *umuntu* is a bearer of intrinsic dignity implies that we owe him/her recognition respect. This is the kind of respect that tracks and responds to ontology, i.e., if one has the valuable nature associated with the capacity for virtue, we owe them recognition respect. This is an equalising kind of respect because it respects one merely because they are human characterised by the relevant ontology, and all those with the same ontology are due equal recognition. If, on the other hand, the agent excels in her actions and character, in terms of manifesting *ubuntu*, we owe them appraisal respect. This is the kind of respect that tracks performance/excellence. This is the kind of respect that comes in degrees, the more one does well, the more respect we owe them, and *vice versa*.

## Conclusion

To conclude this chapter, it might be important to give the reader a clearer account of Ubuntu ethics as self-realisation or perfectionist ethics. We noted that Ubuntu ethics has three components, *umuntu* (a person), *ubuntu* (is a person), and moral relationalism (through other persons). *Umuntu* is important because he/she is the bearer of intrinsic dignity and he/she bears this dignity because she possesses the capacity for virtue.

The perfectionist or the self-realisation element prescribes that *umuntu*, as the moral agent, has the duty to develop the inner quality of his/her nature, the capacity for virtue. The positive development of the capacity for virtue amounts to the emergence of *ubuntu* or personhood. To have *ubuntu* denotes the development of a humane disposition, which expresses itself via pro-social attitudes and behaviours such as kindness, generosity, friendliness, and so on.

We also noted several crucial elements associated with *ubuntu* as the final good. We noted that a balanced interpretation of Ubuntu ethics should recognise its self-regarding (moral individualism) and other-regarding (moral relationalism) elements. The goal of perfection involves the agent developing his/her capacity for virtue (self-regarding aspect) and this goal can only be learned, exercised, and realised in the context of being-with-others. We also noted that the importance of *umuntu*, as a bearer of intrinsic and inalienable dignity, and the goal of acquiring *ubuntu* (personal perfection) are individualistic aspects of Ubuntu as a moral theory. The importance of social relationships, as the only context, for learning and exercising social virtues, or *ubuntu*, represents the relational or communitarian aspect of Ubuntu ethics.

We also interpreted Ubuntu as a perfectionist moral theory in terms of human dignity. We noted that *umuntu* bears intrinsic dignity and the positive development of the capacity to virtue amounts to the emergence of *ubuntu*, or achievement dignity. Finally, we also considered the question of how we should relate to the value of *ubuntu*, as the final good. Is *ubuntu* the kind of value that we should promote, honour, or satisfice? We suggested that Ubuntu ethics commitment to human dignity and social relationships aligns *ubuntu*, as the final good, as the kind of value that we ought to satisfice.

The next chapter turns to political theory.

## Notes

1 We should note the difference between *intrinsic* and *final* value. Intrinsic value refers to the source or location of the value of a thing. It denotes that the value of some object is internal to it, or it's a function of some aspect of the object itself. The value of beauty is intrinsic in the sense described above. When we refer to some value as final, we indicate that it is the moral goal to aspire towards and pursue, and the attitude with which we should pursue it is one that values to object being pursued for its own sake. On some accounts of morality, well-being ought to be pursued for its own sake. It is a valuable good to pursue as an end.
2 The reader should carefully note the distinction between Ubuntu ethics and *ubuntu*, as introduced and discussed in the previous chapter. Ubuntu ethics refers to African moral philosophy, or the African axiological view, whereas *ubuntu* refers to the goal, or the final good. The relation between Ubuntu ethics and *ubuntu* is that the former prescribes the latter as the final good.

3  Note, for example, three influential scholars of African ethics ground morality on some aspect of human nature. Gyekye and Wiredu grounds it on human interests or needs, and Metz grounds it on the capacity for friendliness (see Wiredu, 1992; Metz, 2007; Gyekye, 2010).
4  This paragraph should not be wrongly read to suggest that ethical naturalism is the same as humanism. Ethical naturalism simply refers to the general approach to morality that grounds it on some natural property. Humanism is one example of ethical naturalism in as far as it grounds morality on a specific natural object, specifically human nature.
5  I hope the reader keeps in mind the distinction between the *patient-centred* and *agent-centred* normative notions of a person. The previous chapter focusing on *umuntu* embodies a patient-centred notion of personhood, which accounts for value in terms of certain descriptive feature(s) of our nature, specifically the capacity for virtue that accounts for human dignity. The focus of this section and chapter is the agent-centred notion of a person, which I consider to be tantamount to *ubuntu* or excellence of character.
6  In my view, I distinguish between Ubuntu and *ubuntu*. My view is that *ubuntu* is equivalent to the agent-centred notion of personhood. I highlight this point because it is easy to reduce Ubuntu to personhood, which would be wrong and misleading. Ubuntu represents African philosophy, and *ubuntu* or personhood is one aspect of it, specifically an aspect of its ethical theory.
7  This is a distinction that is typically expressed in terms of the *ontological* and *normative* concepts of personhood in the literature in African philosophy.
8  I imagine some readers might resist the idea that Ubuntu ethics can be characterised in any way as egoistic. The concern might be that Ubuntu has no place for selfishness, and it tends to focus on the importance of the community. In the sub-section, below, dealing with the themes, 'moral individualism' and 'moral relationalism, I anticipate and respond to this kind of objection. It should suffice for now to note that Ubuntu ethics repudiates selfishness (where the agent acts at the expense of another or does not consider another at all when they act), but it does recognise and endorse self-interest as an important ethical plank (see van Niekerk, 2007). The self, *umuntu*, as both a moral agent and a moral patient, must be aware of their self-interest, chief amongst which involves their duty to perfect their own humanity. A person pursues *ubuntu*, in part, because it is good for him/her to attain such a moral character.

## References

Behrens, K. (2010). Exploring African Holism with Respect to the Environment. *Environmental Values* 9: 465–484.

Behrens, K. (2013). Two 'Normative' Conceptions of Personhood. *Quest* 25: 103–119.

Biko, S. (1979). *I Write What I Like*. San Francisco, CA: Harper & Row.

Bujo, B. (1998). *The Ethical Dimension of Community: The African Model and the Dialogue between North and South*. Translated by C. Namulondo. Nairobi: Pauline's Publications Nairobi.

Byron, M. (2004). *Satisficing and Maximising: Moral Theorists on Practical Reason*. Cambridge: Cambridge University Press.

Colenso, J. W. (1861). *Zulu-English Dictionary*. Pietermaritzburg: P. Davis.

DeVries, E. (1966). *Manin Community: Christian Concern for the Human in Changing Society*. New York, NY: Association Press.

Dorsey, D. (2010). Three Arguments for Perfectionism. *Noûs* 44: 59–79.
Dzobo, K. (1992). Values in a Changing Society: Man, Ancestors and God. In K. Gyekye and K. Wiredu (Eds.), *Person and Community: Ghanaian Philosophical Studies*, vol. 1. Washington DC: Council for Research in Values and Philosophy, 223–242.
Etieyibo, E. (2017). Ubuntu, Cosmopolitanism, and Distribution of Natural Resources. *Philosophical Papers* 46: 139–162.
Gade, C. (2011). The Historical Development of the Written Discourses on Ubuntu. *South African Journal of Philosophy* 30: 303–329.
Gyekye, K. (1992). Person and Community in African Thought. In K. Gyekye and K. Wiredu (Eds.), *Person and Community: Ghanaian Philosophical Studies*, 1. Washington, DC: Council for Research in Values and Philosophy, 101–122.
Gyekye, K. (1997). *Tradition and Modernity*. New York, NY: Oxford University Press.
Gyekye, K. (2010). African Ethics. In E. N. Zalta (Ed.), *The Stanford Encyclopedia of Philosophy*. Accessed 16 January 2013. http://plato.stanford.edu/archives/fall2011/entries/african-ethics.
Hughes, G. (2011). The Concept of Dignity in the Universal Declaration of Human Rights. *Journal of Religious Ethics* 39: 1–24.
Hurka, T. (1993). *Perfectionism*. New York, NY: Oxford University Press.
Ikuenobe, P. (2006). The Idea of Personhood in Chinua Achebe's Things Fall Apart. *Philosophia Africana* 9: 117–131.
Ikuenobe, P. (2017). The Communal Basis for Moral Dignity: An African Perspective. *Philosophical Papers* 45: 437–469.
Korsgaard, C. (1983). Two Distinctions in Goodness. *Philosophical Review* 92: 169–195.
Lutz, D. (2009). African Ubuntu Philosophy and Global Management. *Journal of Business Ethics* 84: 13–328.
Matolino, B. (2009). Radicals Versus Moderates: A Critique of Gyekye's Moderate Communitarianism. *South African Journal of Philosophy* 28: 160–170.
May, T. (2014). Moral Individualism, Moral Relationalism, and Obligations to Non-Human Animals. *Journal of Applied Ethics* 31: 156–168.
Mayer, P. (1980). *Black Villagers in an Industrial Society: Anthropological Perspectives on Labour Migration in South Africa*. Cape Town: Oxford University Press.
Mbigi, L. (2005). *The Spirit of African Leadership*. Randburg: Knowers.
McNaughton, D. and Rawling, P. (1992). Honoring and Promoting Values. *Ethics* 102: 835–843.
Menkiti, I. (1984). Person and Community in African Traditional Thought. In R. Wright (Ed.), *African Philosophy: An Introduction*. Lanham: University Press of America, 171–181.
Menkiti, I. (2004). On the Normative Conception of a Person. In K. Wiredu (Ed.), *Companion to African Philosophy*. Oxford: Blackwell Publishing, 324–331.
Metz, T. (2007). Toward an African Moral Theory. *The Journal of Political Philosophy* 15: 321–341.
Metz, T. (2009). African and Western Moral Theories in Bioethical Context. *Developing World Bioethics* 10: 49–58.
Metz, T. (2010). Human Dignity, Capital Punishment and an African Moral Theory: Toward a New Philosophy of Human Rights. *Journal of Human Rights* 9: 81–99.

Metz, T. (2013). Two Conceptions of African Ethics in the Work of D. A. Masolo. *Quest* 25: 7–15.
Metz, T. (2022). *A Relational Moral Theory: African Ethics in and Beyond the Continent.* Oxford: Oxford University Press.
Michael, L. (2014). Defining Dignity and Its Place in Human Rights. *New Bioethics* 20: 12–34.
Mokgoro, Y. (1998). Ubuntu and the Law in South Africa. *Potchefstroom Electronic Law Journal* 1: 1–11.
Molefe, M. (2015). A Rejection of Humanism in the African Moral Tradition. *Theoria* 143: 59–77.
Molefe, M. (2017). Critical Comments on Afro-Communitarianism: The Community Versus Individual. *Filosofia Theoretica* 6: 1–22.
Molefe, M. (2019). *An African Philosophy of Personhood, Morality and Politics.* New York, NY: Palgrave Macmillan.
Molefe, M. (2020). Solving the Conundrum of African Philosophy Through Personhood: The Individual or Community? *Journal of Value Inquiry* 54: 41–57.
Molefe, M. (2021). *Partiality and Impartiality in African Philosophy.* New York, NY: Lexington Books.
Munyaka, M. and Motlhabi, M. (2009). Ubuntu and Its Socio-Moral Significance. In F. Murove (Ed.), *African Ethics: An Anthology of Comparative and Applied Ethics.* Pietermaritzburg: University of Kwa-Zulu Natal Press, 324–331.
Murove, F. (2014). Ubuntu. *Diogenes* 59: 36–47.
Nyembezi, C. S. (1963). *Zulu Proverbs.* Johannesburg: Witwatersrand University Press.
Onah, G. (2013). The Meaning of Peace in African Traditional Religion and Culture. Accessed 8 April 2013. http://www.afrikaworld.net/afrel/goddionah.htm.
Oyowe, A. (2014). Fiction, Culture and the Concept of a Person. *Research in African Literatures* 45: 42–62.
Oyowe, O. A. (2021). *Menkiti's Moral Man.* New York, NY: Lexington Books.
Pauw, B. A. (1975). *Christianity and Xhosa Tradition: Belief and Ritual Among Xhosa-Speaking Christians.* Cape Town: Oxford University Press.
Ramose, M. (2002). The Ethics of Ubuntu. In P. Coetzee and A. Roux (Eds.), *The African Philosophy Reader.* New York: NY: Routledge, 324–331.
Rodegem, F. (1967). *Precises De Grammaire Rundi.* Bruxelles: Story-Scienta.
Rosen, M. (2012). *Dignity: Its History and Meaning.* Cambridge, MA: Harvard University Press.
Samkange, S. (1975). *The Mourned One.* London: Heinemann Educational.
Shutte, A. (2001). *Ubuntu: An Ethic for the New South Africa.* Cape Town: Cluster Publications.
Slote, M. (1989). *Beyond Optimising: A Study of Rational Choice.* Cambridge: Harvard University Press.
Slote, M. and Pettit, P. (1984). Satisficing Consequentialism. *Proceedings of the Aristotelian Society, Supplementary Volumes* 58: 139–163+165–176.
Sulmasy, D. (2008). Dignity and Bioethics: History, Theory, and Selected Applications. In E. Pellegrino (Ed.), *The President's Council on Bioethics, Human Dignity and Bioethics: Essays Commissioned by the President's Council.* Washington, DC: President's Council on Bioethics, 469–501.
Tutu, D. (1999). *No Future Without Forgiveness.* London: Rider.

van Niekerk, J. (2007). In Defence of an Autocentric Account of *Ubuntu*. *South African Journal of Philosophy* 26: 364–368.

Wall, S. (2012). Perfectionism in Moral and Political Philosophy. *Stanford Encyclopaedia of Philosophy*. Accessed 10 March 2019. http://plato.stanford.edu/archives/win2012/entries/perfectionism-moral/.

Wiredu, K. (1992). Moral Foundations of an African Culture. In K. Wiredu and K. Gyekye (Eds.), *Person and Community: Ghanaian Philosophical Studies*, vol. 1. Washington, DC: The Council for Research in Values and Philosophy, 192–206.

Wiredu, K. (1996). *Cultural Universals and Particulars: An African Perspective*. Indianapolis, IN: Indiana University Press.

Wiredu, K. (2009). An Oral Philosophy of Personhood: Comments on Philosophy and Orality. *Research in African Literatures* 40: 8–18.

# 3 Ubuntu Ethics and Politics

## Introduction

This chapter elucidates a political theory associated with Ubuntu ethics. The reader should properly locate this chapter as a contribution to African normative political theory. My primary aim in this chapter involves articulating a theoretical account of a *good* society. Note, this chapter does not aim merely to describe a state or a government; instead, it aims to provide an Ubuntu-based account of "the *proper* purposes of government – so that we can decide on the *best* political arrangements for society" (Pettit, 1991: 2). The previous chapters, one and two, looked at values associated with *umuntu*, specifically, those of human dignity and human excellence (*ubuntu*). The previous chapters offered a micro-ethical analysis, i.e., they give an account of the good (human life) as it relates to the individual or individual-to-individual relations. Our analysis indicated that a good human life is a function of *umuntu*, as the moral agent, developing his/her intrinsic value (the capacity for virtue) to be characterised by *ubuntu*, or a humane disposition.

This chapter operates at a macro-ethical level. Its focus is at the institutional level, which concerns socio-political structures that regulate our collective lives. The purpose of this chapter consists in philosophically explaining how the values associated with *umuntu* of human dignity and *ubuntu* ought to regulate the social institutions to ground a decent/good society, or the best political arrangement of society. This chapter constructs a normative political theory anchored on the twin values of *umuntu* (human dignity) and *ubuntu*. I will associate the value of *umuntu* (human dignity) with the negative requirement that a good society is one that does not humiliate its citizens. I will associate the value of *ubuntu* with the requirement to provide basic needs that are a precondition for the emergence of a robust agent that can actually be expected to pursue it. In the final analysis, I will propose that a good society, or best political arrangements in terms of a suitable government, is one that does not humiliate its citizens (in as far as it respects *umuntu* as a bearer

DOI: 10.4324/9781003514213-4

of human dignity) and provides for their basic needs (in as far as it creates conducive conditions for the emergence of *ubuntu*).

To give an account of an Ubuntu-inspired political vision, or a good society, or what I will call *political morality*, this chapter will make three broad theoretical interventions in the literature on Ubuntu and political theory in African philosophy. Firstly, the chapter will contest the dominant vision in African political thought that insists on defining a good society in terms of human rights. I will provide *prima facie* considerations to supersede rights-based interpretations of African political morality. Specifically, I will criticise attempts in African philosophy, namely, Afro-communitarian radical and moderate political theories of a good society. Whilst I find these influential theories' espousal of rights problematic, I find their commitment to the idea of the common good that embodies a duty-based political theory a vital plank for constructing a plausible African political theory (Menkiti, 1984; Gyekye, 1997). I propose an Ubuntu-based account of a good society or political morality that is grounded on two values definitive of it, namely, *umuntu* (or human dignity) and *ubuntu* (human excellence). These two values, in my view, entail a political system and vision that is diametrically opposed to human rights (see Molefe, 2017; 2019).

The second intervention in accounting for a good society is anchored on the primary value of human dignity. The philosophical intervention should be understood as generally providing a negative account of a good society. In it, I will propose a dignity-based interpretation of a good society, which imagines a good society as one that does not humiliate its citizens. I consider humiliation to essentially involve the violation of human dignity. The notion of humiliation will be tethered to the idea of human dignity to offer a political vision of a robust or even a decent society. The chapter will specifically consider the question concerning the kinds of socio-political conditions, in terms of social institutions that regulate and frame our collective existence as citizens and members of society, that *ought not* to characterise our existence. The proposal will be – we must not live under social conditions or a government that humiliates *umuntu*, a human being, or degrade him/her from his/her status of human dignity. To account for a negative interpretation of Ubuntu's political morality, I draw my inspiration from Avishai Margalit's (1996) brilliant book *The Decent Society*. The book provides a theoretical template to construct a negative account of good social institutions.

The third intervention is anchored on the value of *ubuntu*. This intervention provides a positive account of a good society. It considers and proposes a needs-based account of a good society, where the state, or a good government, has a duty to provide basic goods that are necessary and urgent for the emergence of a robust human being (or moral agent), which is a pre-condition for the possibility of the pursuit and acquisition of *ubuntu*. African philosophers' emphasis on the idea of the common good, construed in terms of basic goods or needs, which we may also understand in terms of Odera Oruka's *human minimum*, will inform the positive account of a good society. A good society provides its citizens with certain essential and basic needs, which are necessary for the emergence of a robust agent, one that can pursue *ubuntu*.

The aim of this chapter is to explicate the political vision of a good society associated with Ubuntu ethics. The aim is to give the reader a snapshot of a good society, it will not defend this vision, at least not in this book. The chapter is divided into four major sections. The first section considers attempts to provide an Ubuntu-based account of a good society, which anchors it on the primacy of human rights. It considers two influential African political theories of rights as instances of a good society, namely, radical and moderate communitarianism. It further provides considerations that repudiate rights-based interpretations of African political thought. The second section provides a negative account of a good society, where it relies on the idea of a decent society as the basis for political morality. I will suggest that a good society is one that does not humiliate or degrade the human dignity of its citizens. The value of human dignity anchors the negative account of African political theory, where humiliation is a function of degrading human dignity.

The third section will offer a positive account of a good society, which will pivot on the value of *ubuntu*. It imagines positive and empowering conditions necessary for the emergence of *ubuntu*. It associates the emergence of *ubuntu* with the state providing the common good. I will account for the idea of the common in terms of basic needs or the human minimum. I will argue that a good society is one that provides the basic needs necessary for the emergence of a robust agent. The final section will respond to a criticism raised by Bernard Matolino and Wenceslaus Kwindingwi in their essay 'The End of Ubuntu' (Matolino and Kwindingwi, 2013). I respond to this objection to give the reader a sense of the robustness of Ubuntu as a moral and political theory.

Below, I begin by repudiating attempts to ground African political morality on human rights.

## Ubuntu, Human Rights and a Good Society

The concept of personhood, as presented by Ifeanyi Menkiti (1984), is central not only to moral theory but also to political morality. That is, personhood has not only been associated with an ethical theory of a virtuous agent, the human good (which we noted that it accounts for in terms of achieving human excellence or *ubuntu*), but it has also played a crucial role in shaping debates about a just or good society. Kwame Gyekye (1992: 102) captures the connection between the notion of a person and political morality in this fashion, "The type of social structure or arrangement evolved by a particular society seems to reflect – and be influenced by – the public conceptions of personhood held in that society". In Gyekye's view, a conception of personhood held in a particular culture/society informs the type of social structure they would consider suitable and useful for our existence as human beings. The suggestion is that there is a connection between a conception of a person and a good society, i.e., personhood can guide us in our imagination of the basic organisation of society that is decent or suitable for human existence. Hence, the tendency and debates in African political philosophy have been to derive a conception of political morality from a conception of a person. The debates in African philosophy have revolved around the view that if a theorist would advance a plausible conception of personhood, they are most likely to arrive at a plausible conception of a good society.

I begin by considering how the theory of radical communitarianism accounts for a good society.

## Radical Communitarianism

Two pioneering scholars of personhood and political theory in African philosophy have articulated conceptions of personhood and subsequently associated them with a particular theory of a good society. Ifeanyi Menkiti (1984) articulates the normative concept of a person, the agent-centred notion of a person, and associates it with a particular type of social structure (see also Menkiti, 2004). Menkiti's view of personhood tethered to a conception of political morality is described in the literature in terms of radical communitarianism (Gyekye, 1992; Matolino, 2009; Oyowe, 2013, 2014)[1]. This view embodies a radical/extreme conception of a good society for two reasons (at least this is a common accusation levelled against it in the literature).

Firstly, the literature notes that Menkiti proposes a conception of a person that places an exaggerated emphasis on the role of the community in the definition of a person. For example, Menkiti (1984: 180) summarises his view of personhood as follows, "… in the African view, it is the community which defines the person as person, not some isolated static quality of rationality, will, or memory". The concern with such a view is that it does not consider the place and role of the individual and individual capacities in its conception of a person (Gyekye, 1997; Eze, 2009).

Secondly, it is described as a radical vision of a good society because of the political morality associated with it, or that follows from its conception of a person. The objection from the literature is that Menkiti's vision of political morality does not take rights seriously (Oyowe, 2013, 2014; Molefe, 2016). Note the kind of social structure Menkiti (1984: 180) associates with a conception of a person, "The African understanding of human society ... adopts ... what I have called 'collectivities in the truest sense' there is assumed to be an organic dimension to the relationship between the component individuals". In Menkiti's view, a community is not an artificial invention of human genius; it is a natural aspect of human existence. A human being is born in the community, and he/she requires the community to emerge and to function in the world. Menkiti (1984: 181) goes further to associate this conception of a person-in-relation-to-community to have the following implications for political morality,

> In the African understanding, priority is given to the duties which individuals owe to the collectivity, and their rights, whatever these may be, are seen as secondary to their exercise of their duties.

Notice that Menkiti sharply contrasts an individual-based and a community-based political morality. The former places priority on the rights of individuals and the latter on the duty to the collectivity, or community, which I will refer to as the common good. Menkiti's view has been roundly rejected and described as radical in the literature for assigning a secondary status to human rights (Metz, 2012; Molefe, 2016). It is worth noting, however, that Menkiti's view does consider rights to have a place and some role in a conception of a good society; however, it is a limited one. I find Menkiti's prioritisation of duties over rights to be a promising approach to African political morality, but I find his espousal of human rights to be problematic – I will suggest below why I reject the inclusion of human rights in a conception of a good society.

I turn now to moderate communitarianism.

## *Moderate Communitarianism*

Consider also Gyekye's (1997) moderate communitarianism as a political morality. Gyekye articulates a political morality based on what he considers a plausible conception of a person. For him, a plausible conception of a person ought to have a place for both human nature's communal and individual features. In other words, a correct conception of a person must reckon with the sociality and individuality of the human agent. The basic insight behind Gyekye's view of a person is that it recognises that a human being is naturally a member of some society. Hence, relationality is a defining aspect of his/her existence or personhood. He insists, however, that the individual, in her own right, as he/she is, possesses individual features like rationality, volition, and so on. Gyekye (1992: 111) rightly notes that the community does not create these individual features, rather, it discovers them, and it (the community) plays a crucial role in developing them. The community's role in developing these individualistic features, such as rationality, does not render them any less features that, strictly speaking, belong to the individual and that can only be expressed by the individual. Hence, a robust conception of personhood and political morality must equally consider the place of these two defining features of a person, her relational and individual features.

Gyekye makes two crucial proposals to construct a political morality. Firstly, he associates the social/relational and the individual features that define a person with certain moral values. He associates the social or relational aspect of a person with the value of the *common good* and associates the individualistic features with *human dignity*. By the 'common good', Gyekye (2010) appears to be referring to the basic needs that every individual requires to be able to lead a proper and satisfactory human life, such as access to public health (Gyekye seems to be reducing a satisfactory life to one characterised by well-being). The idea of the common good captures the pervasive belief or assumption in African thought that there is a basket of goods that each human being requires to emerge and function as a normal human being. Concerning the individualistic features, Gyekye (1997: 63) places a prime on "the mental feature" of autonomy, which accounts for the value of human dignity associated with human beings. He uses the idea of human dignity to denote the individual's moral worth that he/she has in her own right because of the individualistic properties he/she has and specifies autonomy as the relevant metaphysical capacity[2].

According to Gyekye, the twin values associated with human nature embody a particular conception of social justice or a good society. A good society operates based on equally recognising the twin values of the common good and human dignity (Gyekye, 1997: 41). On the moderate vision of a good society, it is characterised by creating conditions generally conducive to human well-being. I associate the common good with human well-being because, for Gyekye, human well-being is "the master-value" (Gyekye, 2004: 51). In other words, the cluster of goods represented through the idea of the common good are designed to ensure the well-being of human beings, i.e., a basket of goods that are necessary for a human life to go well (Gyekye, 1997, 2004). In Gyekye's view of a just society, the state has to provide conditions and resources that conduce towards human well-being. Otherwise, the state is weak or unjust.

The value of human dignity is also central in moderate communitarianism. According to Gyekye, a good society is one that recognises the importance of human dignity (Muade, 2023). In his account of human dignity, he appears to prefer Kant's autonomy-based account of human dignity to be compatible with African thought or moderate communitarianism. For Gyekye, the autonomous aspect of our nature cannot be set at nought or reduced by the community, no matter how important the community and its goals are. Human dignity captures an inalienable value of a human being that society and the state must reckon with and protect as much as possible. To protect the valuable state of our autonomous feature that secures our human dignity, Gyekye (1992) associates it with human rights. Concerning human rights, Gyekye (1992: 114) makes the following remark,

> Rights belong primarily and irreducibly to individuals; a right is the right of some individual. Yet the supposition that communitarianism will have no places or very little, if at all, for rights will be false both in theory and practice, especially in the case of ... moderate communitarianism.

Rights serve as moral-political means to recognise and protect human dignity to ensure a decent existence (Hughes, 2011). One central aspect of the kinds of rights that Gyekye has in mind seems to play the crucial role of protecting individuals from the threats that a communitarian polity may impose on individuals. The role associated with human rights involves their negative function, which is associated with what we described as *constraints* in Chapter 1. This role involves setting moral-political parameters that protect the individual from unjustified and arbitrary interventions by the community. For example, the cultural community may not necessarily be in favour of homosexuality, and they may be tempted to tamper with the individual's sexual orientation and preferences. Human dignity is important as it will serve as a constraint in as far as the individual's choice of sexual preference is not harming anyone, and he/she should not be interfered with or harmed for expressing their sexual preferences towards a competent consenting adult. The political good, expressed via human rights that recognise and protect individual autonomy, trumps the cultural community's actions or activities that seek to undermine the individual's human dignity.

Hence, according to moderate communitarianism, a just social order operates on the dual values of the common good and human dignity. The common good imagines the positive duties (and a host of social goods) the state must provide to secure human well-being. The value of human dignity (through human rights) imagines negative duties to protect the human individual from possible interferences, threats, and harms from society.

Note the difference between the radical and moderate communitarian visions of a good society. The difference between the two is rooted in their differing conception of personhood. Because it conceives of personhood as entirely defined by the community or relationality, the former places a prime on the common good without jettisoning human rights; it allocates a secondary status to them. The latter, because it equally values individuality and relationality, elevates human rights to the status of the common good, where they function to protect the individual value of human dignity. Like radical and moderate communitarianism, the approach I will favour emphasises the common good, but it excludes human rights altogether as a part of a robust African political morality.

I considered the two visions of a good society because I believe both correctly capture the tenor and orientation of African political morality, accentuating the importance of duties in responding to human needs. The duties associated with the common good are directed towards ensuring that all human beings have access to the basic needs required to survive and thrive in society. I reject these theories for their unjustified inclusion of human rights in African political morality. Below, I outline reasons why I reject human rights.

*Rejection of Human Rights*

In this section, I dispute the relevance of human rights in African political thought. Space and the purpose of this chapter and book will not permit an extensive argument for setting rights aside. Three observations will suffice to suggest why rights should not be at home in an African morality. Firstly, note that both radical and moderate communitarianism fail in their attempts to include rights in African political morality. I use the strong word *fail* because it occurs to me that they do not seem to correctly grasp the status, power, and role of rights in political theory. Note that Menkiti assigns a secondary status to human rights. Menkiti ranks rights second to the primacy of duties. Gyekye's moderate communitarianism appears to take rights seriously, but ultimately, it also ranks them, in certain instances, as secondary to duties particularly when there is a clash. Note this comment by Gyekye (1992: 116–117),

> ... although it is conceivable, as has already been explained, that the communal structure will allow the exercise of individual rights, *yet it can be expected that communitarianism would not suggest to individuals incessantly insist on their rights* ... Individuals would not have a penchant for, an obsession with, insisting on their rights, knowing that insistence on their rights could divert attention to duties they, as members of the communal society, strongly feel towards other members of the community.

In another place Gyekye goes beyond merely noting that Afro-communitarian limits the individual in terms of them insisting on their rights. He explicitly states that,

> All these considerations elevate the notion of duties to a status similar to that given to the notion of rights in Western ethics. African ethics does not give short-shrift to rights as such; nevertheless, it

does not give obsessional or blinkered emphasis on rights. *In this morality duties trump rights, not the other way around, as it is in the moral systems of Western societies.*
(Gyekye, 2010: n.p., emphasis mine)

Ultimately, it seems that Gyekye, as much as he wants to elevate rights and duties to have the same status, places a greater emphasis and significance on duties. The concerning feature of both radical and moderate communitarianism is that human rights, particularly when construed as natural rights, do not appear to be the kinds of moral-political instruments that can be secondary, as Menkiti and Gyekye regard them.

The literature on political morality tends to associate rights with a trumping or peremptory function (although this function is not absolute), i.e., rights tend to be so powerful that they set aside even social policy to promote the common good. It does not seem to be in the nature or function of human rights to be assigned a secondary status without diminishing their essence in morality and politics (Donnelly, 1982). Note, Joel Feinberg's (1970: 621) classical essay 'The Nature and Value of Human Rights' provides one of the most useful and insightful accounts of both the nature and function of rights in political morality in this fashion. He begins by distinguishing two types of societies, one without human rights and one with them. He observes that citizens and societies without regards lack something morally and politically significant, the ability to make claims against others. He comments in this regard concerning the rights,

> ...there is no doubt that their characteristic use [human rights] and that for which they are distinctively well suited, is to be claimed, demanded, affirmed, insisted upon. They are especially sturdy objects to 'stand upon,' a most useful sort of moral furniture. Having rights, of course, makes claiming possible; but it is claiming that gives rights their special moral significance.

Rights are moral-political properties that empower an individual to make claims against the state and others in society. These (rights-claims) are very powerful claims when legitimate. These are the kinds of claims, as Feinberg informs us, that the agent is empowered to demand (it is not a request), insist upon (it is not a favour), and affirm (the state has to protect and ensure them). It is in the nature of rights, as claims or entitlements, that one must insist on them if they are to appreciate their power and enjoy them. The individual may relinquish their right, even the act of relinquishing them is his/her right. The community, be it cultural or political, cannot unduly force or demand that the agent give up his right without violating or undermining him/her. It is precisely the idea of rights as claims against the state and society which renders them unsuitable to take a secondary status.

An example of how rights might frustrate the common good is the case of a property owner (the right to private property), which she acquired legitimately. She may justifiably frustrate the government's plans to build houses for the poor on land identified as suitable for a building programme if the property owner refuses to sell; she has a right to it, she has a right not to sell, and a right is a powerful thing to have (all things being equal). Hence, rights are not suited to take a secondary status if they are to do their political work of protecting and empowering individuals against the state and other members of society. I note that African scholars must decide if they want rights as claims and entitlements in their political morality. If they do, they must accept rights for what they are and entail, which does not seem compatible with them playing a secondary or remedial role.

Finally, Jack Donnelly (1982), a leading human rights scholar, writes about analysing the concept of human rights in non-Western cultural contexts and makes fascinating observations concerning human rights in non-Western cultures. He begins by distinguishing right, as a property of an action or conduct, where some agent's actions may be described as right, from a right (a human right), as a property of a human being or an entitlement. He defines human rights as entitlements that the right-holder has against the duty-holder (Donnelly, 2009). If I have a right to my property, it creates duties for others to respect me and my property and allow me space to do as I see fit with it. Rights, as entitlements, at least in Donnelly's analysis, are interpreted within the naturalist framework, where we have them merely because we are human, and they (rights) function to protect us from harm and empower us to function and flourish as human beings (Donnelly, 2009).

In his analysis of non-Western cultures (including African cultures), he observes that the idea of human rights as entitlements is generally absent in the moral systems of these societies. He is not criticising these societies for not having human rights; instead, he is describing the characteristic features of their political morality. He is not using the West as a standard of morality. Rather, he contrasts it with other valid forms of imagining morality and politics. Donnelly rightly observes that the political morality prevalent amongst African cultures recognises the primacy of human dignity and prescribes duties as the best way to recognise, protect, and respect it (human dignity). Simply put, African political morality marries the idea of human dignity to duties to create a conducive society for human survival and flourishing.

This way of interpreting African morality is consistent with Ubuntu ethics. Ubuntu ethics tends to imagine agents, not in terms of what is due to them as a primary focus; instead, the primary focus (from the agent's perspective) is on what is due to others (Molefe, 2017, 2018). Ubuntu ethics emphasises what we owe to others in two related ways. On the one hand, it requires us to imagine ourselves as already caught up in social relationships with others – 'I am because we are', where participation and contribution towards sustaining harmonious relationships is a priority (Mbiti, 1970). To be human, or to be fully human, essentially requires the agent to connect and interact with others. On the other hand, part of what is contained in this connection is positively responding to another's condition of need and vulnerability, i.e., to foster a healthy dependence or interdependence amongst agents (Wiredu, 1992; Gyekye, 2010). Hence, when scholars describe the agent that has *ubuntu*, one that has a humane disposition, it almost always is in terms of what he/she does to connect with and benefit others – he/she is kind, loving, generous, friendly, patient, tolerant, and so on.

If Ubuntu ethics imagines a connected moral agent that responds to others positively, human rights imagine a totally different kind of moral agent. The attitude associated with rights as entitlements or making claims against others, characteristic of the moral philosophy, psychology, and language of human rights, is generally absent in Ubuntu ethics (see Molefe, 2017, 2018). Rights are essentially confrontational, where the agent claims or demands against another, whereas Ubuntu ethics seeks to extend itself to another by responding to their state of need and to foster a culture of interdependence. The general incompatibility between the language of rights and *ubuntu* leads me to look elsewhere for a robust political morality in African thought.

I turn now to the second intervention.

## Ubuntu, a Good Society and Humiliation

In a brilliant book, *The Decent Society*, Margalit (1996) proposes what may be described as a duty-based political theory. The theory is political because it aims to spell out an account of the conduct of the state and/or social institutions towards its citizens – it focuses on macro-ethical issues. Firstly, it distinguishes a just and a decent society. A just society tends to account for social justice in terms of human rights, where rights are a decisive or primary moral-political consideration in accounting for an acceptable social arrangement. A decent society does not consider rights as a crucial feature of ethics and politics. In fact, Margalit does not even have a place for human rights in his political vision of a decent society. This consideration is important because it is consistent with my goal and interpretation of a non-rights-based interpretation of a good society in African thought. Ubuntu can embody a purely duty-based political morality that responds to the human condition of need (Molefe, 2018).

Secondly, since Margalit is after a decent society, it is crucial to clarify the concept of 'decent' in his political thought. A decent society is one that does not humiliate citizens. By society, he considers the state and its subsidiaries, which we may refer to as social institutions that regulate our shared and/or collective lives. Margalit (1996: 1) defines social institutions in "abstract" and "concrete" terms. The abstract focuses on the laws, policies, and rules regulating a society. The apartheid government of South Africa, in terms of its laws of racism, is an example of abstract element of an indecent society. The concrete element focuses on the agents' "actual behaviour" that advances the goals and mandates of social institutions like police brutality against black people in America (Margalit, 1996: 1). Given this definition of a decent society in terms of social institutions, our typical nation-states or countries could be construed as social institutions in Margalit's sense since they have both elements the abstract and concrete.

A decent society is one whose social institutions do not humiliate citizens. Humiliation, according to Margalit (1996: 5), involves "injury to self-respect, that is, to the respect [the] human being deserves for the very fact of being human". In my view, a useful way to interpret what Margalit refers to as an 'individual's sense of self-respect' is to understand the idea in terms of injuring a person's moral worth or his/her sense of self-worth. The expression of self-worth is the explanatory moral and ontological ground for self-respect, i.e., self-respect arises in relation to an individual's moral worth. Hence, in my reading, we may construe humiliation to involve degrading treatment towards a being with moral worth. We may associate moral worth with human dignity because of Kant's distinction between price and worth (Kant, 1996). My interpretation of humiliation in terms of degrading human dignity is informed and motivated by a crucial observation in the literature on human dignity, where Kaufmann et al. (2011: 4) identify a distinct sense of dignity that they refer to as "the negative approach" to human dignity.

This comment by Kaufmann et al. (2011: 2) is informative regarding the relationship between humiliation and dignity that I am proposing here,

> ... we propose to look more closely at dignity violations and adopt what we call a 'negative approach to human dignity'. The contributions to this book can all be said to proceed from philosopher Avishai Margalit's insight that we learn most about human dignity when we look at its violations and focus on what it means for people to be degraded, humiliated and wronged in many other ways.

Drawing from Margalit's insight on the idea of a decent society and humiliation, contributors to Kaufmann et al.'s volume propose to account for human dignity in terms of how it can be fundamentally degraded or undermined by human behaviour or certain human-engineered conditions. Central to this approach to human dignity is that it does not start from some abstract principle; instead, it considers concrete cases of human violation, which they describe in terms such as "humiliation and degrading treatment, torture and war, poverty and slavery" (Kaufmann, 2011: 1). This approach to human dignity argues that another useful way to make sense of our moral worth as human beings, as bearers of human dignity, is in terms of when we are treated less than our status of being human. A treatment from a moral agent that reduces or inferiorises us from our human status can be characterised as degrading and humiliating. Hence, the essence of humiliating treatment is that it dehumanises us by inferiorising us as beings of dignity (Oliver, 2011; Sangiovanni, 2017).

The inferiorisation of human beings from their rightful status can take different forms, such as *instrumentalisation* (treating one merely as a means to the agent's end without regard to her humanity, be it in terms of her volition, conation, or agency), *objectification* (treat a human being as if it they are an object or a thing, which has no interests, goals, and so on), or *infantilisation* (treating an adult as if they are a child) (see Sangiovanni, 2017). Rape is a perfect example of an inferiorising treatment, where an adult woman who has a choice regarding with whom and when to have sex is treated less than a human being to be reduced to an object or instrument to merely satisfy the sexual desires of another without considering her interests and consent. The individual's human ability to make choices and express her desires is wholly ignored and violated in this violent and degrading act of rape.

Considering the negative idea of human dignity, we can define humiliation (as described by Margalit as injuring an individual's sense of self-worth or human dignity) as the inferiorisation of a human being from their human status. The humiliation can be a function of both conditions and/or human action/conduct, so long as such conditions can be traced back to some laws, rules, and policies of the institution or agent's direct actions that undermine a human being as a bearer of dignity (Margalit, 1996). In other words, if an individual finds him/herself under what may appear to be inferiorising conditions, like when a terrible flood would render one homeless, we do not have an instance of humiliation. At best, it is just an unfortunate and unsuitable situation (at least this is how we understand the term humiliation in political morality). Humiliation, strictly speaking, is associated directly with the social institution's rules and their agents' conduct towards human beings, and their status of dignity (Margalit, 1996). Hence, a decent society does not humiliate its citizens, which involves operating based on laws, rules, and policies that are consistent with recognising and empowering human beings as bearers of human dignity. A society is not decent when it humiliates its citizens, i.e., disregards and degrades them in their status as human beings.

Why do I believe that Ubuntu ethics should be defined in terms of non-humiliation or as a decent society? Two reasons justify the move to define Ubuntu's political morality in terms of the idea of a decent society, which society is characterised by the prime value of non-humiliation as its defining hallmark. Firstly, Margalit's political theory of a decent society operates based on the distinction between a just and a decent society. Just societies tend to place a prime on human rights as a decisive moral-political consideration in political morality. In Margalit's sense, a decent society places a prime on the value of non-humiliation. I believe that Ubuntu should be construed as a decent society because attempts to ground it on human rights have failed dismally in the literature on African philosophy. Whereas scholars may continue their quest after a rights-based interpretation, I believe that Ubuntu ethics is open to an interpretation that does not consider human rights as a decisive value to account for a good society. The quest towards a non-rights-based interpretation of Ubuntu ethics motivates this view, more so when there are *prima facie* reasons that supersede rights in African thought.

For another consideration, which ties Ubuntu ethics and Margalit's moral and political vision of a decent society, Margalit (1996: 64) believes that the concept of honour lies at the heart of the axiological and political system that informs the idea of a decent society. The point Margalit is making is that there is a difference between political visions grounded on honour and those grounded on human rights. There are moral cultures whose primary moral considerations revolve around honorific terms. I believe that Ubuntu ethics and the values that characterise it take the form of honour rather than rights. The idea of *ubuntu* and/or personhood are honorific terms. When someone says, 'I have a right to this property' or when we say 'she has a right to this property', the moral language involved here is one of demands and claims against others. It is a language loaded with moral and legal power that the agent has over others (Feinberg, 1970; Donnelly, 2009). Whereas, when we say that some agent has *ubuntu* or is a person, we approve and praise her for living a decent human life. To be called a person or to be declared to have *ubuntu* amounts to a special kind of recognition; it is tantamount to being honoured for one's quality of actions, character, and humanity.

Hence, we note that there is a conceptual and moral difference between politics grounded on honour and rights. The language of rights identifies an agent as a legitimate maker of claims against others, whereas the language of *ubuntu* approves the agent for positively relating and benefitting others. The moral attitude of honour is pervasive amongst African cultures. Consider, for example, amongst the Nguni people, when you meet someone and greet them, which is somewhat of a cultural duty, one expresses their greeting '*sawubona*'. The word '*sawubona*' literally means, we see you. The underlying idea is that you cannot meet a human being and behave like you are walking past an animal or an object with no value. The greeting, *sawubona*, is an expression of honour by recognising another human being, rightfully, as a human being. It is the consistency amongst these two traditions in terms of espousing moral systems of honour that justifies my interpretation of Ubuntu political morality in terms of non-humiliation.

Considering the above, we note that Ubuntu may be construed to embody a political morality that enjoins us not to humiliate citizens. A good society recognises and is responsive to the human condition of dignity. The primary goal of a decent society involves honouring human beings since they possess the capacity for virtue. It can honour them by removing socio-political and economic conditions that do not treat them as bearers of intrinsic dignity. Consider the following two practical cases to provide concreteness to the kind of political morality associated with Ubuntu ethics construed as a decent society.

Firstly, consider apartheid as a paradigm example of an indecent society. The laws that define the mandate of such a state and the tasks it assigns to its agents are characteristically humiliating towards most of its citizens (I have South Africa as the point in case). By humiliation, remember, I have in mind the idea of degrading or inferiorising a human being from their human status and regarding and treating them as less, such as a child, an animal, or a thing. Apartheid, as a social institution, legalised racism and created a socio-political and economic culture that promoted racism as a defining feature of society. The white section of the population enjoyed the full privileges of citizenship and even more. They had access to decent education, public health, reservations of jobs (which simultaneously excluded black people from certain jobs), and suitable settlement conditions with functioning infrastructure. On the other hand, the black majority could not vote, could not fully and freely access job opportunities, were subjected to an inferior form of education called Bantu Education, generally did not have access to decent public health, police meted out arbitrary and unjustified violence, killings, kidnappings, and torture to create a culture of fear and terror. The social conditions under which black people lived and the treatment they received from the institutions were generally of a humiliating kind.

For another example, consider the post-apartheid Marikana massacre in South Africa. Marikana is a community of miners next to the town of Rustenburg in the North West province of South Africa. In 2011, workers for the mine of Lonmin engaged in an unprotected (illegal) strike, where they were protesting the indecent living conditions and meagre salaries. The humiliating conditions, in terms of the settlement and salary, were vestiges of the erstwhile colonial and apartheid regimes compounded by an ineffective black government of the African National Congress. The miners were demanding a basic salary increase of R12,500. The culture of low and indecent salaries in South Africa is connected to the history of the discovery of minerals in Kimberley (1867) and gold in Johannesburg (1886), the dispossession and removal of black people from arable land to small and infertile land and the introduction of hut tax to force men to leave their families to earn a wage so they can pay their taxes. The demand for a living wage is the call for a decent society to ensure that people work under appropriate conditions and earn a living wage[3].

One leading scholar of Ubuntu ethics, Thaddeus Metz (2017), reflected on the aftermath of the massacre (the police shot and killed 34 people) and the Farlam Commission that was established to investigate the matter (Office of the President of South Africa, 2012). In the final analysis, Metz argues that "that the government should have taken resolute steps towards seeking reconciliation of a specific sort that I show follows from [Ubuntu] interpreted as an ethical theory" (Metz, 2017: 287). Whilst the suggestion of reconciliation is a good one, it is hardly sufficient to address the historical economic legacy of cheap black labour associated with the indignity associated with poor housing conditions and low salaries. Over and above reconciliation, in fact, prior to thinking of reconciliation, Ubuntu ethics should emphasise redressing humiliating conditions on the part of the vestiges of the history of colonialism, apartheid, and capitalism; it must also challenge the state and current employer to create favourable employment conditions for its workers in terms of decent settlement and salaries. Promoting reconciliation whilst the humiliating conditions persist fails to properly regard *umuntu* as a bearer of intrinsic dignity (Molefe and Magam, 2019).

In the context of South Africa and Africa in general, Ubuntu ethics would urge us to consider redressing the socio-structural features of our existence that are humiliating. The protracted structural inequality and unemployment in South Africa and many other parts of Africa amount to existing under humiliating conditions. Unemployment is humiliating because the human agent has no avenue to pursue gainful employment, where they can develop their talents, pursue a career, and afford their own lives, and it tends to lead to pauperism and hunger. Some parts of the continent have lived under dictatorships and military governments, where citizens live in constant fear and terror. Political participation is of a limited and horrid kind, where political opponents are persecuted, kidnapped, or even killed. Minorities have no say in making policies that shape their lives and futures. Ubuntu ethics requires us to remove conditions that do not adequately regard human dignity. We require social institutions that operate based on laws and agents that recognise and protect citizens from degrading conditions of existence.

Next, we consider the positive part of Ubuntu's political morality.

## Ubuntu, a Good Society and the Human Minimum

The previous section, which imagines a good society as a decent one, construed an Ubuntu-based political morality to involve the removal of humiliating conditions by focusing on the removal of conditions that are unsuitable for *umuntu* as a bearer of human dignity. In other words, the focus on political morality in terms of a decent society focused on creating conditions consistent with recognising and protecting human dignity. This section constructs political morality by considering the value of *ubuntu*, the final good. The question I am pursuing here concerns theoretically constructing the political conditions that are conducive for *umuntu* to be able to pursue *ubuntu*. What conditions must persist before we can legitimately expect *umuntu*, as a moral agent, to pursue *ubuntu*? The basic assumption here is that it would be amiss and unjust for a society to expect agents to pursue *ubuntu* when they live under conditions that do not enable *umuntu* to do so (Molefe and Magam, 2019).

Ubuntu ethics prescribes that the moral agent should pursue *ubuntu* (Gyekye, 1992; Tutu, 1999). This moral expectation or even prescription cannot be arbitrary or unreasonable. For example, not all social conditions are suitable for the emergence of *ubuntu*. We cannot, for example, expect *umuntu* to pursue *ubuntu* under the harsh, cruel, and humiliating conditions of slavery and to be a child soldier. There is a way that slavery reduces and stunts *umuntu* that the only legitimate moral emotion is that of pity and sympathy, but not that he/she should pursue *ubuntu* under such morally paralysing conditions. Certain conditions, such as slavery, torture, and kidnapping, can disempower *umuntu* so radically that we may not expect him/her to pursue *ubuntu*.

I am aware that my discussion of conditions that are unsuitable for the emergence of *ubuntu* may come across as if they are stated in absolute terms. I know there will never be perfect conditions where all that is required for human flourishing will be readily and abundantly available. The point I am making, however, in the context of articulating an Ubuntu-based political morality, is that certain oppressive conditions are not conducive to the emergence of *ubuntu*. I am not precluding the possibility that such conditions could actually be where we can see the development and manifestation of *ubuntu*. Consider the famous heroic actions of Harriet during slavery, where she liberated scores of enslaved people into freedom. Her life and the lives of many anti-slavery and liberation movements in Africa are instances of how, *umuntu*, even in unbecoming circumstances, could still manifest *ubuntu*. Contexts of injustice, such as slavery, should never serve as a standard for imagining suitable socio-political conditions that must attend decent human existence. Whereas we must applaud the courage of people like Gandhi, Martin Luther King, and Mandela, amongst others, we should equally see how social injustice de-focused them from thinking about what and how they ought to live their own lives on their terms.

The question that arises considering the above comments about unsuitable conditions for human existence might urge us to develop a positive account regarding socio-political conditions that are suitable or necessary for the emergence of *ubuntu*. Martha Nussbaum imagines political morality in this fashion, "the task of the 'basic structure' of society to put in place the necessary conditions for a minimally decent human life, a life at least minimally worthy of human dignity, expressive of at least minimal respect" (2008: 359–360). The aim of this section, therefore, involves defining the basic structure that will ensure necessary conditions for a minimally decent human life, i.e., basic conditions that are designed to recognise, protect, and empower *umuntu* to thrive and excel as a moral agent in the world.

In African philosophy, scholars describe the general conditions that are suitable for the emergence of ubuntu in terms of the *common good* or what they describe as *humane conditions* (Wiredu, 1992; Gyekye, 1997; Ilesanmi, 2001; Masolo, 2004). Gyekye, one of the scholars who has throughout his career in African political thought, sheds some light on the idea of the common good (Gyekye, 1992, 1995, 1997, 2004). I will draw from his writings on African political morality to explain the idea of the common good, which ultimately involves the provision of basic needs for the proper or ordinary functioning of a human being as a moral agent that can pursue certain ends, particularly *ubuntu*.

Firstly, note Gyekye (2004: 57, emphasis mine) informs us that the common good "is a fundamental human good". He also states, "the common good, then, is identical with human good". The common good refers to a cluster of goods that are necessary for human beings as such, it is an embodiment of fundamental human good. The idea of 'fundamental', as in 'a fundamental human good', points to their basic or essential status, suggesting that human life would be unfortunate, miserable, and undesirable without the common good. Secondly, note Gyekye (1992: 117) associates the idea of the common good with the politics of duty,

> [African political morality, or communitarianism] Concerned, as it is, with the common good or the communal welfare, the welfare of each and every member of the community, communitarianism will, perhaps undoubtedly, consider duty as the moral tone, as the supreme principle of morality. By 'duty', I mean task, service, conduct or function that a person feels morally obligated to perform in respect of another person or other persons.

Note that Gyekye associates the idea of the common good with the provision of 'material' or goods that are necessary for the welfare of every member of society (I will say something about what this idea of 'the welfare of every member of society' below). He proceeds to connect the idea of the common good and the idea of duty to suggest that we need to construe African political morality in terms of the supreme value of duty. To regard duties to be supreme suggests all other values, including rights, are secondary, which accentuates why I insist on duty-based politics. Though

Gyekye considers duties at individual-to-individual relations, I will imagine them at a political level, i.e., as they relate to the duties that social institutions, such as the state and their functionaries, have towards their citizens. The idea of duty refers to the moral service or task social institutions and their agents must contribute to secure the well-being of each and every member of society. The duties that Gyekye (1992: 119) associates with the common good are expressed in terms of relational, social, or other-regarding virtues such as "solidarity, interdependence, cooperation, compassion, and reciprocity" and so on.

Thirdly, we consider what Gyekye means when he refers to the common good to embrace the kinds of goods that secure the welfare of every member of society. Gyekye (2004: 45) defines the idea of the common good to refer to "essential [goods] for the ordinary or basic functioning of the human person in a human society". Moreover, he understands the common good to involve "the provision for the social conditions which will enable each individual person to function satisfactorily in a human society" (Gyekye, 1992: 116). In another place, Gyekye associates the common good with the "basic goods that every individual person needs in order function satisfactorily" (Gyekye, 2004: 54). A meaningful or robust human existence involves being able to engage in certain functions. By functions, Gyekye seems to refer to the range of things we can do and be as human beings. Hence, Gyekye associates the provision of the common good with satisfactory or ordinary human function. We can conclude that the common good refers to the basic goods, which refers to social conditions and benefits, which are conducive for human being to emerge as a robust agent that can pursue a range of activities and goals in the world. I consider 'satisfactory or ordinary function' to denote agency.

The political morality associated with the common good is one that aims to provide conditions that enable the development of a robust agent. The duties associated with a decent society, or its social institutions, involve the provision of basic needs, or the common good for the development of such a robust agent. Furthermore, Gyekye's reference to basic/essential goods or social conditions to enable ordinary human functioning can be rightfully associated with duties that respond to human needs, which are necessary for the emergence of a robust agent. For example, Gyekye (2004: 48, emphasis mine) is very specific that the common good refers to "the *basic needs* that can be said to be intrinsic to the functioning of human beings as human beings". Basic needs are connected directly to the emergence of a robust agent. Note that these basic needs are described as *intrinsic* to human development and function.

The suggestion that these needs are intrinsic to human function captures the salient view of the human condition in African philosophy, which tends to ontologically and axiologically associate it with need. The human condition is essentially characterised by natural inadequacy or self-insufficiency, which places a human being from the cradle to the grave in a position where they need the help of their kind to varying degrees (Wiredu, 1992; Engmaan, 1992; Molefe and Allsobrook, 2021). These needs arise due to a variety of reasons, such as "embodied existence", which necessitates access to "food, clothing, shelter, and other material needs" (Engmann, 1992: 89). Beyond these existential needs, there is what we may refer to as the human or moral need, which is connected to moral development and function of a human being as a moral agent in relation to the pursuit of *ubuntu*. The moral need is connected to developing our essential and moral capacity for virtue so we can pursue *ubuntu*.

Remember, Ubuntu ethics prescribes the acquisition or development of *ubuntu* as the final good. The agent is expected or required to pursue *ubuntu*. This requirement, however, implies that human beings must have developed a robust agency, which is a pre-condition to engage in the task of nurturing *ubuntu*. The common good, therefore, imagines institutional arrangements, or the provision of basic goods, which are necessary for the emergence of a robust agent, which is a pre-condition for the pursuit of *ubuntu*. Notice this comment about the importance of meeting moral or basic needs,

> The needs that matter are bounded by the idea of the necessary, the essential, the indispensable, or the inescapable. Furthermore, if the needs are not met, we are unable to do anything much at all and certainly are unable to lead a recognisably human life. Meeting the morally relevant needs is central to our abilities to function as human agents.
> 
> (Brock, 1987: 15)

The same insight about fundamental, moral, or basic needs is expressed in African philosophy by Odera Oruka in terms of what he describes as the *human minimum*. Oruka's (1997) vision of a good society essentially involves the provision of the human minimum. The idea of the human minimum points to a need-based approach to a good society, where we have institutions that operate on the moral logic of providing basic human needs that are central to our abilities to function as human agents (see Graness, 2015). Jonathan Chimakonam (2020: 106) interprets Oruka's human minimum as a needs-based approach as follows,

> ... the sum of basic provisions a state must guarantee to its citizens, without which it is impossible for citizens to act rationally. In the absence of this human minimum, Oruka argues that people will suffer from compromising poverty that will rob them their dignity and self-worth, making it impossible for them to act rationally most of the time.

The underlying idea behind Gyekye's and Brock's idea of basic needs or Oruka's interpretation of the idea of the human minimum is that without the provision of certain basic and necessary human goods, it is almost impossible for a robust human agent to develop that can achieve valuable functions in the world. The acquisition of *ubuntu* depends precisely on the ability to exercise these valuable functions. The provision of the basic goods or the human minimum is crucial to achieving what Oruka refers to as "a more humanised life on Earth", where a human being can do and be all that is expected of him/her, including the acquisition of *ubuntu* (Oruka, 1997: 85). According to Oruka, lack of access to the human minimum amounts to a dehumanised form of existence. The kind of dehumanization involved is characterised by a human agent that is not properly development in that she may not be able to function like a normal human being. Hence, what is at stake in the provision of the basic needs, or the human minimum, is the "preservation of the value of humanity in the universe" (Oruka, 1997: 85).

Different scholars would specify different lists of what would count as basic needs. Gyekye (2004) could be interpreted to distinguish between survival and trans-survival needs. The former comprehends "material needs" such as "hunger, thirst and sex" (Gyekye, 2004: 45–57). The latter comprehends needs associated with our social existence such as "security, peace, safety, love, recognition, status, honor, influence, happiness, solidarity, human creativity and productivity, motherhood, fatherhood, success and prosperity" (Gyekye, 1992: 44). Oruka (1997: 100) specifies security, subsistence, and health as necessary for the development of rational agents or what Oruka describes in terms "of thoughtful existence". Another scholar of needs, Sarah Clarke Miller (2012: 41–42), suggests her list of basic needs comprises "Nutrition and water; Rest; Shelter; Healthy Environment; Bodily Integrity; Healing; Education; Attachments; Social Inclusion, Participation, and Recognition; Play and Security". Miller (2012: 17) further notes, "Meeting the basic needs of each and every individual is necessary to establish, maintain, or restore a human agent".

My point is not to settle the question of which list is most plausible the basic needs. The question of identifying and defending a plausible list lies outside this chapter's scope. The point regarding a good society we appreciate considering above is that social institutions have the duty to ensure the provision of certain basic needs for the sake of the emergence and maintenance of a robust human agent. Though Oruka accounts for a robust agent in terms of thoughtful existence or rationality, I find Miller's (2012) conception of it to be more promising as she accounts for it in terms of emotional, relational, and rational capacities. To have *ubuntu* surely does have something to do with thoughtful existence, but it does comprehend relationality and emotional attunement as well. Hence, the aim of politics, or social institutions, revolves around providing pre-conditions for the emergence of a robust agent. A good society provides the common good for the development of the human agent. It is unjust and unfair to expect *umuntu* to achieve *ubuntu* where we have not provided suitable conditions for developing a robust agent to pursue valuable functions in the world.

## Why Ubuntu/*ubuntu* Should Not End

Matolino and Kwindingwi (2013) argue that Ubuntu is no longer relevant for modern, secular, and multi-cultural societies. In fact, they argue that Ubuntu, like other narratives of return, is bound to fail because the prevailing socio-political conditions are not suitable for it. Below, I outline two considerations or reasons that suggest why we should not take Matolino and Kwindingwi's call for the end of Ubuntu/*ubuntu seriously*.

Firstly, given my distinction between Ubuntu and ubuntu, it is not entirely clear what the object of the criticism is. It seems misguided to require the end of either. If one calls for the end of Ubuntu, it would seem that the years that African philosophers spent clarifying and defending Ubuntu, or African philosophy, were in vain. To call for the end of Ubuntu is tantamount to denying African people reason, the ability, amongst others, that is necessary to do philosophy (Ramose, 1999). We may not be happy with the state of both the oral and written archive of Ubuntu, philosophy, or even its (ab)use by politicians, but that is not reason enough to call for its end. If, on the other hand, the target is *ubuntu*, then the criticism is still misplaced. The call of *ubuntu* is for human agents to be humane, i.e., to have kindness, mercy, love, friendliness, and so on. It would strike me strange that anyone would not want to see individuals and social institutions like governments abandoning such crucial values/virtues. In short, we insist that Ubuntu should not be abandoned because it is an instance of African philosophy. We insist that *ubuntu* should not be abandoned because it embodies virtues that would render human life tolerable and meaningful.

It is possible that Ubuntu/*ubuntu* has been used wrongly by the ruling black elite to further their political agendas. It is even possible that philosophers and other scholars of African thought have failed to provide a coherent account of it. Even this state of affairs would not justify the hasty view that we should get rid of Ubuntu/*ubuntu*.

Secondly, my interpretation of Ubuntu ethics suggests that it would be totally wrong to end Ubuntu/*ubuntu*. My interpretation identified three crucial components of Ubuntu ethics, namely, *umuntu* and the value of human dignity, *ubuntu* and its manifestation via pro-social behaviours, and the importance of social relationships. To defend the view that we should not end Ubuntu/*ubuntu*, I will focus on the first component of Ubuntu ethics, *umuntu* and human dignity. The call to end

Ubuntu/*ubuntu* is philosophically problematic because it fails to recognise that at the core of it is a call to recognise *umuntu* as a bearer of intrinsic value, which imposes on us both negative and positive duties. Ubuntu is about *umuntu*, a human being. Ubuntu offers an African perspective, which could be useful in moral-political philosophy and policy formulation, to engender socio-political conditions anchored on the recognition and protection of *umuntu*.

The philosophy of Ubuntu and its requirement for the agent to acquire *ubuntu* is primarily about *umuntu*. Now more than ever the prime place that Ubuntu associates with *umuntu* should be carefully considered, clarified, and defended given the terrible continued record of human violations and degradations worldwide. The need to recognise, protect, and promote *umuntu* as a bearer of human dignity is even more pressing in a world that promises so many avenues to humiliate and deny human beings basic needs for their survival and functioning as human beings. In the context where humanity and the conditions of their existence are precarious, it is important that we strengthen the call inherent in Ubuntu ethics to seek to create a world conducive for *umuntu* to live and thrive. Social and political conditions associated with slavery, colonisation, unjustified wars, oppression, and the marginalisation of women and children must be extirpated to create conducive forms of existence for all humanity and the environment.

It is in the spirit of human dignity associated with *umuntu* that I sincerely believe that it is wrong to call for the end of Ubuntu. The nexus between the philosophy of Ubuntu and *umuntu* is reason enough to repudiate the call for its end. Ubuntu presents us with a picture of *umuntu* as a bearer of intrinsic value, *umuntu* as having the potential to acquire *ubuntu*, and *umuntu* as existing and thriving in relationships. It is the centrality of *umuntu* that informs my view to reject the call for its end. The call inherent in Ubuntu ethics is not one that requires us to go back to some past, as Matolino and Kwindingwi seem to suggest. Instead, Ubuntu ethics is a call that requires us as moral agents to creatively imagine a world and the future where *umuntu* is truly recognised and respected. Ubuntu ethics is not a historical project, but it is a live and continuing project for humanity to find itself, unfold itself, and flourish.

## Conclusion

This chapter articulated an Ubuntu-based philosophical picture of a good society. To explain Ubuntu-based political morality, the chapter made three moral-theoretical interventions on the literature on political morality. Firstly, it began by providing reasons to move away from interpretations of African political morality that include or place a prime on human rights. Secondly, it proposed an Ubuntu-based political morality in terms of a decent society, where a good society is one whose institutions do not humiliate citizens. We defined humiliation as conditions or conduct that treat human beings less than their value and status of dignity. Humiliation involves institutions' inferiorising persons by subjecting them to conditions (structural unemployment, homelessness, and so on) and actions (torture and kidnappings). Non-humiliation is a call to remove things that injure *umuntu* as a being of dignity.

The final intervention offered a positive account of a good society, which placed emphasis on specifying conditions that must hold before we can legitimately expect moral agents to pursue *ubuntu*. We accounted for suitable conditions in terms of the common good, which we interpreted to comprehend basic needs or the human minimum necessary for the emergence of a robust agent. A good society enables human beings to develop as robust agents, which is a pre-condition for the pursuit of *ubuntu* as the most important and valuable moral end. We concluded the paper by responding to the criticism that calls for the end of Ubuntu/*ubuntu*. We noted that Ubuntu/ubuntu is about *umuntu*, a human being, and so long as human beings are alive, the ethic of Ubuntu is relevant as it imposes on us the duty to recognise and respect *umuntu*.

## Notes

1 It is worth noting that Menkiti has never used or endorsed this classification of his political morality.
2 I am aware that Gyekye's exposition in relation to human dignity can be associated with three distinct theories of human dignity. One will find two distinct religious theories: (1) we have dignity because we are children of God and (2) we have dignity because we are created in God's image. The fourth theory is one Gyekye draws from Kant's moral theory, which accounts for it in terms of the capacity for autonomy (Muade, 2023).
3 The following newspaper articles provide context: (1) https://www.sahistory.org.za/article/marikana-massacre-16-august-2012, (2) https://mg.co.za/news/2022-08-16-the-mail-guardians-first-documentary-is-on-marikana-this-is-why/, and (3) https://www.dailymaverick.co.za/marikana-massacre-miners-police-killings-anniversary/.

## References

Brock, G. (1987). *Meeting Needs*. Princeton, NJ: Princeton University Press.
Chimakonam, J. (2020). Is the Debate on Poverty Research a Global One? A Consideration of the Exclusion of Odera Oruka's 'Human Minimum' as a Case of Epistemic Injustice. In V. Beck, H. Hahn and R. Lepenies (Eds.), *Dimensions of Poverty*, Cham: Springer, 97–114.
Donnelly, J. (1982). Human Rights and Human Dignity: An Analytic Critique of Non-Western Conceptions of Human Rights. *The American Political Science Review* 76: 303–316.

Donnelly, J. (2009). *Human Dignity and Human Rights*. Denver, CO: Josef Korbel School of International Studies.
Engmann, J. (1992). Immortality and the Nature of Man in Ga Thought. In K. Wiredu and K. Gyekye (Eds.), *Person and Community: Ghanaian Philosophical Studies*, vol. 1. Washington, DC: The Council for Research in Values and Philosophy, 153–159.
Eze, M. (2009). What Is African Communitarianism? Against Consensus as a Regulative Ideal. *South African Journal of Philosophy* 27: 386–399.
Feinberg, J. (1970). The Nature and Value of Rights. *The Journal of Value Inquiry* 4: 243–457.
Graness, A. (2015). Is the Debate on 'Global Justice' a Global One? Some Considerations in View of Modern Philosophy in Africa. *Journal of Global Ethics* 11: 126–140.
Gyekye, K. 1992. *Person and Community. Ghanaian Philosophical Studies, 1.* Washington, DC: Council for Research in Values and Philosophy.
Gyekye, K. (1995). *An Essay on African Philosophical Thought: the Akan Conceptual Scheme*. Philadelphia, PA: Temple University Press.
Gyekye, K. (1997). *Tradition and Modernity: Philosophical Reflections on the African Experience*. New York, NY: Oxford University Press.
Gyekye, K. (2004). *Beyond Cultures: Perceiving a Common Humanity, Ghanaian Philosophical Studies*. Accra: Ghana Academy of Arts and Sciences.
Gyekye, K. (2010). African Ethics. In E.N. Zalta (Ed.), *The Stanford Encyclopedia of Philosophy*. Accessed 16 January 2013. http://plato.stanford.edu/archives/fall2011/entries/african-ethics.
Hughes, G. (2011). The Concept of Dignity in the Universal Declaration of Human Rights. *Journal of Religious Ethics* 39: 1–24.
Ilesanmi, O. (2001). Human Rights Discourse in Modern Africa: A Comparative Religious Perspective. *Journal of Religious Ethics* 23: 293–320.
Kant, E. 1996. *Groundwork of the Metaphysics of Morals*. Translated by M. Gregor. Cambridge: Cambridge University Press.
Kaufmann, P., Kuch, H. M., Neuhauser, C. and Webster, E. (2011). Instrumentalisation: What Does It Mean to Use a Person? In P. Kaufmann, H. M. Kuch, C. Neuhauser and E. Webster (Eds.), *Humiliation, Degradation, Dehumanization: Human Dignity Violated*. New York, NY: Springer, 67–84.
Margalit, A. (1996). *The Decent Society*. Cambridge, MA: Harvard University Press.
Masolo, D. (2004). Western and African Communitarianism. In K. Wiredu (Ed.), *Companion to African Philosophy*. Oxford: Blackwell Publishing, 483–498.
Matolino, B. (2009). Radicals Versus Moderates: A Critique of Gyekye's Moderate Communitarianism. *South African Journal of Philosophy* 28: 160–170.
Matolino, B. and Kwindingwi, W. (2013). The End of Ubuntu. *South African Journal of Philosophy* 32: 197–205.
Mbiti, J. (1970). *African Religions and Philosophy*. New York, NY: Doubleday.
Menkiti, I. (1984). Person and Community in African Traditional Thought. In R. Wright (Ed.), *African Philosophy: An Introduction*. Lanham, MD: University Press of America, 171–181.
Menkiti, I. (2004). On the Normative Conception of a Person. In K. Wiredu (Ed.), *Companion to African Philosophy*. Oxford: Blackwell Publishing, 324–331.

Metz, T. (2012). An African Theory of Moral Status: A Relational Alternative to Individualism and Holism. *Ethical Theory and Moral Practice: An International Forum* 14: 387–402.
Metz, T. (2017). An Ubuntu-Based Evaluation of the South African State's Responses to Marikana: Where's the Reconciliation? *Politikon* 44: 287–303.
Miller, S. (2012). *The Ethics of Need: Agency, Dignity, and Obligation.* New York, NY: Routledge.
Molefe, M. (2016). Revisiting the Debate between Gyekye-Menkiti: Who Is a Radical Communitarian? *Theoria* 63: 37–54.
Molefe, M. (2017). Critical Comments on Afro-Communitarianism: The Community Versus Individual. *Filosofia Theoretica* 6: 1–22.
Molefe, M. (2018). Personhood and (Rectification) Justice in African Thought. *Politikon* 45: 352–367.
Molefe, M. and Allsobrook, C. (2021). *Towards an African Political Philosophy of Needs.* New York, NY: Palgrave Macmillan.
Molefe, M. and Magam, N. (2019). What Can Ubuntu Do? A Reflection on African Moral Theory in Light of Post-Colonial Challenges. *Politikon* 46: 311–325.
Muade, E. (2023). Moderate Communitarianism and Human Dignity. In E. Pellegrino (Ed.), *Human Dignity in an African Context.* New York, NY: Palgrave Macmillan, 107–126.
Nussbaum, M. (2008). Human Dignity and Political Entitlements. In A. Schulman (Ed.), *Human Dignity and Bioethics: Essays Commissioned by the President's Council*, Washington, DC: President's Council on Bioethics, 351–380.
Office of the President of South Africa. (2012). Terms of Reference: Commission of Inquiry into the Tragic Incidents at or near the Area Commonly Known as the Marikana Mine in Rustenburg, North West Province, South Africa. *Government Gazette* No. 35680, 12 September. Accessed 17 October 2023. http://www.justice.gov.za/legislation/notices/2012/20120912-gg35680-nor50-marikana.pdf.
Oliver, S. (2011). Dehumanisation: Perceiving the Body as (in)Human. In P. Kaufmann, H. M. Kuch, C. Neuhauser and E. Webster (Eds.), *Humiliation, Degradation and Dehumanisation: Human Dignity Violated.* New York, NY: Springer, 85–98.
Oruka, O. (1997). *Practical Philosophy.* Nairobi: East African Publishers.
Oyowe, A. (2013). Strange Bedfellows: Rethinking Ubuntu and Human Rights in South Africa. *African Human Rights Law Journal* 13: 103–124.
Oyowe, A. (2014). An African Conception of Human Rights? Comments on the Challenges of Relativism. *Human Rights Review* 15: 329–347.
Pettit, P. (1991). *Contemporary Political Philosophy.* New York, NY: Macmillan Publishing House.
Ramose, M. (1999). *African Philosophy Through Ubuntu.* Harare: Mond Books.
Sangiovanni, A. (2017). *Humanity Without Dignity: Moral Equality, Respect, and Human Rights.* Cambridge: Harvard University Press.
Tutu, D. (1999). *No Future Without Forgiveness.* New York, NY: Random House.
Wiredu, K. (1992). Moral Foundations of an African Culture. In K. Wiredu and K. Gyekye (Eds.), *Person and Community: Ghanaian Philosophical Studies*, vol. 1. Washington, DC: The Council for Research in Values and Philosophy, 192–206.

# Index

a person is a person through other persons, 3, 7–9, 19, 20, 21, 25, 30, 32, 38, 44, 51, 57, 59, 60
abortion, 24, 41, 42
Africa 3, 4, 6, 11–13, 16, 82, 86
African cultures 4–7, 32, 46–48, 80, 84
African ethics 2, 3, 4, 15, 21, 23, 30, 45, 47, 51, 59, 60, 67, 79
African philosophy, 4, 6, 10, 12, 13, 14, 16, 20–22, 25, 26, 30, 32, 33, 45, 46, 48, 50, 67, 72, 74, 84, 88, 89, 91, 92
agent-centred, 21, 25, 26, 27, 29, 39, 44, 45, 47, 56, 59, 67, 74
analytic philosophy, 13, 14, 16
animal ethics 24
anthropocentrism, weak anthropocentrism 30
autocentric 1, 46

basic needs 9, 10, 15, 46, 72, 73, 76, 78, 88–91, 93, 94
Behrens 23, 30, 50, 51, 54, 61
Botho 1, 19

capacity for autonomy 34, 94
capacity for virtue 35, 37–39, 43, 54, 55, 58, 59, 64–67, 71, 85, 90
character 1, 6, 23, 25, 27, 29, 44, 48–51, 55, 58, 61, 62, 65, 67, 84
colonisation 5, 7, 93
common good 9, 10, 57, 72, 73, 75–80, 88–90, 92, 94
communitarianism: moderate communitarianism 47, 73, 75–79; radical communitarianism 74
critical humanism 2, 5, 9
cultural community 77

decent society 14, 72, 81–87, 89, 94
degrading 12, 65, 72, 83, 85, 86
dehumanization 91
duties 34, 36, 37, 39, 55, 57, 75–80, 88, 89, 93; other-regarding duties 55, 57; negative duties 24, 77; positive duties 24, 77; special duties 31

egalitarianism 36–38, 43, 65
egoism 16, 56
empowerment 36–38
entitlements 79, 80, 81
epistemicide 5
ethical naturalism 45, 67
excellence 4, 6, 15, 16, 20, 22, 25–28, 38, 45, 46, 48–53, 58, 65, 67, 71–73
extrinsic value 29

*Feta kgomo o tsware motho* 32, 33
final good 15, 21, 44, 45, 53–56, 64, 66, 87, 90
foundation 19, 20, 43, 45, 59

Gade 1, 4, 6, 54
glocal phenomenon 5, 6
good government 72

homosexuality 77
honour 61–63, 66, 84, 85
human minimum 73, 86, 90, 91, 94
human nature 1, 2, 10, 35, 43, 45–47, 51, 53, 54, 56, 57, 67, 76
human rights 5, 10, 72, 73, 75, 77–81, 84, 93
human-centred approach 30
humane(ness) 21, 44, 54–58, 60, 66, 71, 81, 88, 92

## Index

humanism 1, 2
humiliation 9, 15, 72, 73, 81–85, 94

individualistic properties 23, 76
intrinsic value 10, 15, 19, 21, 28, 29, 30, 32, 34–38, 43, 44, 54, 59, 64, 66, 71, 93

macro-ethics 71, 81
Margalit 81–84
master value 76
micro-ethics 71
moral agent 2, 4, 6, 16, 21, 23, 25, 27, 30, 38, 44, 47, 49, 51, 53, 55, 56, 58, 59, 65–67, 71, 72, 81, 83, 87, 88, 90; moral disposition 20, 53; moral egoism 16, 56
moral perfection(ism) 3, 15, 16, 44–47, 51–53, 58, 61, 63–65
moral philosophy 1, 6, 24, 30, 31, 36, 61, 66, 81
moral status 22–30, 37–39, 43, 55
morality 2, 3, 21, 27, 30, 39, 43, 45–51, 53–58, 60–62, 66, 67, 72–76, 78–81, 83–89, 93, 94

naturalist framework 80
needs 88, 90, 91, 93, 94
negative duties 39, 77

Oruka 90, 91

personal identity 3, 75–77, 84
personhood 3, 4, 9, 21–26, 28, 45, 47, 48

primary value 19–21, 26, 39, 43, 72

relational(ism) 39, 44, 55, 57, 59, 61, 65, 66, 68
robust agent 72, 73, 89–92, 94

secondary value 19–21, 39, 43, 44
self-realization 44, 56
sentience 24
*seriti* 3, 9
sexual orientation 77
Shutte 2, 3, 9, 46, 57, 61
social institutions 2, 72, 81, 82, 86, 87, 89, 91, 92
socialization 23
status term 34

ultimate value 19–21
*umuntu* 6–10, 15, 20–45, 48, 53, 59, 64–67, 71, 72, 86–88, 92–94; *umuntu ngumuntu ngabantu* 7–9, 19, 20
utility 3

well-being 2, 9, 20, 51, 61, 66, 76, 89
Wiredu 4, 10, 13, 21, 22, 26, 30, 32, 46, 48–50, 67, 81, 88, 90

value term 35, 38
virtue 4, 6, 9, 10, 15, 16, 20, 22–28, 34, 35, 37, 39, 43–48, 50, 51, 53–55, 58, 64–67, 71, 85, 90